T0209817

Find The G-Spot
Of Your Soul

Move from Lethargic to Ravenous Living

Dr. Marina Kostina

BALBOA.
PRESS
A DIVISION OF HAY HOUSE

Balboa Press books may be ordered through booksellers or by contacting:

Balboa Press
A Division of Hay House
1663 Liberty Drive
Bloomington, IN 47403
www.balboapress.com
1 (877) 407-4847

Because of the dynamic nature of the Internet, any web addresses or links contained in this book may have changed since publication and may no longer be valid. The views expressed in this work are solely those of the author and do not necessarily reflect the views of the publisher, and the publisher hereby disclaims any responsibility for them.

The author of this book does not dispense medical advice or prescribe the use of any technique as a form of treatment for physical, emotional, or medical problems without the advice of a physician, either directly or indirectly. The intent of the author is only to offer information of a general nature to help you in your quest for emotional and spiritual well-being. In the event you use any of the information in this book for yourself, which is your constitutional right, the author and the publisher assume no responsibility for your actions.

Any people depicted in stock imagery provided by Getty Images are models, and such images are being used for illustrative purposes only. Certain stock imagery © Getty Images.

Print information available on the last page.

ISBN: 978-1-9822-1763-1 (sc)
ISBN: 978-1-9822-1767-9 (e)

Balboa Press rev. date: 01/07/2019

Dedication

To all the brave souls who are done feeling lethargic
and are ready to experience a ravenous joyful life
and let their souls set the world on fire.

Acknowledgment

In Russia we have an expression, "Good teachers are expensive".... I want to thank all my "expensive" teachers who seemingly hurt me, abandonded me, betrayed me, or broke my heart. You are my biggest gifts. Thanks to you I found my most important relationship- relationship with myself and my divine. Thanks to you I am fully alive. I know in some incredible way you have been orchestrating my journey back home.

About the Author

Dr. Marina Kostina is a life and business fulfilment coach who helps people break out of their limited, lethargic, "status quo" existence, allowing them to enjoy what she describes as a "ravenous life"–a life filled with passion, pleasure, and playfulness.

An Amazon bestselling author, seven-time recipient of the United States Department of Defense grants, and winner of the BIBO Outstanding Entrepreneurship Award, Dr. Kostina's work has been featured in such prominent media sources as USA Today, Telemundo, Chicago Tribune, and People Magazine, Authority Magazine, Thrive Global, and Buzzfeed.

Highly regarded internationally for her work as a motivational speaker and energy healer, Dr. Kostina guides men and women on their journeys to reclaim the fragmented pieces of their souls, restoring them to a state of wholeness – the state that "allows you to manifest your biggest dreams and create the lifestyle that brings you freedom." For more information visit: www.drmarinakostina.com.

Preface

This book will take you on a rollercoaster ride. You will discover the G-spot of your soul and will get in the flow, gracefully moving from pain to pleasure. In the end you will realize that your sexuality, creativity and spirituality have the same source and only in acceptance of all these aspects of yourself can you find true liberation and joy.

CONTENTS

Chapter 1: Foreplay

"To know yourself as the being underneath the thinker,
the stillness underneath the mental noise, the love, and joy
underneath the pain is freedom, salvation, enlightenment."

-Eckhart Tolle

~ *Goddess Marina* ~

It is 7 a.m., the alarm has gone off and I am out of sorts and in complete exasperation. I cling on to my yoga mat and dread the situation that I am faced with …. I am at the dance studio sleeping on the yoga mat as I cannot afford a real home and the only roof over my head is this studio whose owner graciously offered me as a shelter. I play my happy role well as I get up 30 min before the first class, hiding the evidence of my homeless life, cheering my students with a big smile and a hi-five. No one has any idea… But today is different. My alarm betrayed me and the loud knock in the window caught me completely in shock.

The students are coming in thick and fast and banging on the door - and I am so not ready to face them. I did not wash my face, my hair is a mess… *"How will I get out of this one?"* I am thinking while I am rolling on my yoga mat (aka my bed). My mind is swirling all over and I cannot fathom how to deal with my current situation anymore.

I feel embarrassed considering what an abject failure I am... I almost reached my midlife point and I still do not have anything substantial to show for my endeavors in life. I spent my adolescence in Russia and when my mom brought me to the US to live the *American Dream,* somehow my inner cruise control got set on "survival mode" and got stuck on it ever since. I worked numerous odd jobs to cover the expenses of higher education which culminated in my Ph.D, building roads, cleaning washrooms, serving and bartending at restaurants and ultimately sleep deprived for decades.... After all the struggle, I finally thought that I had made it because I was able to complete my Ph.D. My business was thriving. I got married and moved into the home of my dreams – everything was just falling into place it seemed. Until thatone moment arrived and took it all away: no more family, no more husband, no more home, no friends in proximity (they had moved away in the same year that everything was unraveling), and basically jobless other thana small position as a Zumba instructor at the above mentioned studio.

I was not prepared, no warning shots were fired and suddenly I was back to zero and dare I say, in a worse state than I was in when I moved to the States. I did not have any safety net to fall back on.

"Why did I come here? How could he do this to me? Why did I even get married? I hate this floor..." and suddenly, as I was rolling that mat I realized... that **during all those times of anguish, and numerous pondering about my life, the problems were not outside of me but were innate and self-created.**

FIND THE G-SPOT OF YOUR SOUL

It hit me: As I pushed, persevered, conquered and to an extent succeeded... in the midst of proving my aptitude to others, I never got the space for my own happiness and self-gratification. I was completely bereft of the elements that constituted my pleasure and self-esteem because I was stuck in the maelstrom of obligations and making others content.

As I moved across the world, I needed to settle in, get a degree, a well-paying job and in achieving that, I left out every trace of pleasure from my life. I had become a slave to the survival, to the *"making it in the USA"*. My playful and pleasure-seeking nature was forced to shrink inside and so did my self-worth.

I was suffocating as if I was put in a room which induced claustrophobia. Even though I had had several high paying professions that reflected what I truly loved and had the necessary degrees to back that up, I would assert that it still was not my soul's purpose. I realized that something was missing from my life and hence the perpetual struggle to push and succeed. I would look at other people who easily could attract anything they wished into their lives, but nothing seemed to come my way. I had to struggle my way to topple the patriarchy and constantly persevere in all walks of life. It was truly agitating.

I began to realize that the problem lies with how society views the female gender, how we are all supposed to look according to a standard ...one for all... and many of us, women, spend plenty of time, money and effort to fit into that image that has been created for us by the outside world. In a bid to fulfill others' expectations, our very own unique identity is concealed leaving most of us unhappy and empty and putting us into the struggle and ultimately survival mode.

Even so-called successful women seem to not have space for pleasure in their lives, as we forget that the real essence of femininity is the energy, the ingenuity, pleasure, play, sensuality and the sense of goddessness. They are all needed in a subtle mirage to find our life's purpose.

See, most men can go to work for the sake of earning their sustenance and *"doing deeds",* and will not have any problem doing so but for us women, it is an entirely different ball game. We need something else. We need our souls to be expressed and if that does not happen, no amount of money or incentive can make us content and full. For a woman to be disconnected from her core feminine principles is equivalent to a suicide. We need to be able to create that personal space among ourselves where we can foster growth and happiness.

Society, on the other hand, patronizes us for these feminine principles and cravings. The patriarchy is leading the way in almost all walks of life by way of dominance and strangling merit. Women are deprived of their rights in the areas of pleasure, it is something that we females are dissuaded to achieve from a very early childhood by our elders - and for women, it is generally considered promiscuous even to talk about. While most men are admired and encouraged for their hedonistic lifestyles, for women it is almost a topic of taboo.

I remember growing up in the Soviet Union, my mom and I had to stand in long lines for food and household items. I was five years old. I remember entertaining the crowd of people waiting in line with us. I recall wearing a long skirt and playing with a tamborine, my long hair loose and floating…and I danced. I danced to celebrate my beauty and my femininity—a young girl reveling in her loveliness, my dancing putting smiles on the faces around me, providing a stark contrast to our bleak circumstances. I was happy and full inside, filled with love for myself, and I had so much love inside me to give back. I was powerful, and that was scary to others. As I grew up, instead of gaining admiration and support for my feminine, free-spirited behavior, I heard more and more often to stop being "so darn powerful, so energetic, so brave." From that moment on, I decided to hide my power and focused on my outer achievments, which slowly but surely led me to the moment on that yoga mat--broken and empty, unfulfilled and lost.

It is fascinating how, on some subconscious level, society detected the powerful sexual energy in a little girl, and, fearing it, conspired to make her suppress it. This happens all over the world, and has happened throughout history. For example, women who exuded sexual energy were often labeled as witches. They were condemned by the church, hated by other women, and shunned by men who felt threatened by them. This feminine power was considered a dark, evil force; multitudes of women who posessed it were burned and tortured in public demonstrations, undoubtedly teaching future generations of little girls to repress their sexual vibrancy.

This fear of sexually powerful women exists because sexual energy is the most fundamental energy in human beings--in a sense, it's the force of life itself. It is the wild, intuitive nature within us that does not submit to any laws or outside control. Female sexuality is not darkness; it is an endless source of light; yet, even today, society demands that we suppress this force and extinguish our own light.

I had a dream once that shows exactly what happens to a woman, energy-wise, when she disconnects from her feminine power: I was walking in a dark, magical forest with beautiful flowers and wild animals all around; my heart was full and I did not need anyone else... Suddenly I saw an ugly snake laying on the road hissing at me. Her slimy body (the snake was female) was disgusting, her open mouth and long poisonous tongue taunted me, foreshadowing the most torturous death ever. I overcame my fear and stepped forward. As I moved in closer, the face of the snake started to melt and suddenly I saw tears coming out of her eyes. In shock, I looked back at myself; I could see I'd morphed into a magical being, split down the middle with two faces, each face looking in the opposite direction. All of a sudden I felt a sharp, excruciating pain in my head(s). Deep inside of my tailbone I saw snake-like energy, lights of energy, moving in a beautiful way, yet painfully torn from something bigger; they were like many threads that were torn from a main source...I closed my eyes, moved even closer to the snake, took a couple of deep breaths and... inhaled it! As the snake hit the inside walls of my stomach and traveled along my spine, it transformed into the most beautiful blue light I'd ever seen, shining and sparkling, the split sides of my body re-uniting, turning the two women's faces that had emerged from my head back towards each other, making them one. My headache was gone; my body was now filled with light. I had become the light, shining upon the entire forest, and beyond--to the entire world, dissipating its darkness.

This is what happens to us as women, when we suppress our passion in order to fit into the norms that society creates for us. Our passion lays in wait for us, dormant, like an ugly snake threatening to kill us for not using it properly. Only when we muster the bravery to connect with that passion--to be wild and free and break all the norms--only then are we able to become that light shining in the darkness, like a wondrous lighthouse that brings hope and joy to everything around it. Most of us are just one step away--albeit a difficult step--from living the life of our dreams. Sadly, most of us never take this step.

And this creates a situation where women forget how to dream and aspire. We are trying to serve everybody and over function, and in doing so we forsake our own dreams. Most of the times my clients come to me and complain about not having a clear direction in life. I ask them what their dreams are and they look silent. One girl said she could not smile but that she wanted to smile. I asked her what makes her smile and she could not tell me. How terrifying is that?

I see this all the time in my energy sessions- most adults are devoid of joy, they have forgotten how to play, how to be goofy, fun and spontaneous. They are so stern and serious! These are things that are substituted with the outside elements to fit society and harbor a fake image. We are caught in our own mental prison.

But the fact remains that sensuality, playfulness and the feeling of goddessness come from within. Most women who come to me are ashamed of their bodies compared to men who can have protruding bellies, who go to the washroom not bothering to close the door, who scratch their private parts and they find it perfectly normal. We women, however, are always having a problem and are crippled by insecurities.

Besides, most women have some form of PTSD (Post-traumatic stress disorder), as we have suffered unfairness, misjudgment and a holy guacamole of sexual advances during our lifetime. In order to protect ourselves from these unpleasant circumstances, we leave our feminine energies behind and instead lead with the masculine energy- pushing, competing, protecting, conquering, succeeding... And that is precisely how we miss the flow and stop loving ourselves.

When you connect with your life purpose, you get on the right track, the track to self-discovery and self-worth. Your sense of self expands, all of your doubts and criticisms of others do not matter because you are connected to something bigger than you and become larger than life. You have a message to share with the world and that is precisely why your self-esteem grows.

You start creating *"space"* in your life. Space is not only important for us, but for the opposite gender as well. A woman creates space through her dreams, imagination and creative faculty. For example, if she wants a home in an immaculate condition, she can see and almost feel it and the man is the catalyst that makes her wishes come true. So it is fair to say that the male energies fill the space while the female energies create the space. Even nature has constructed us that way. The male sexual organ fills up the space the female creates.

But how can you create space if you are shrunk inside? When we are not connected with the universal flow, we become hollow and empty which then translates to feelings of resentment. When we are resentful, we tend to blame others; and men become the easy prey. Men despise the fact that they are judged and not embraced by others and they too shrink next to us creating an endless cycle of self-loathing, broken and unhappy relationships...

I would also like to mention that when we forsake our feminine energy, we lose track of our innate gifts and develop the habit of denying our blessings. Our life becomes very bleak – because we came here as a soul to fulfill our higher purpose but if we detach ourselves from our gifts, we betray nature by not living up to what has been expected from us by the universe.

And when we don't live our purpose, the universe gets involved. It starts creating circumstances that demand our shrewd actions and a sensible approach. It involves us in relationships, events, and situations that are at times painful, tragic and difficult. It molds our character to be responsive to perilous situations. It is like a wake-up call because we are pushed and made to persevere to conquer our demons. As only when we are in distress, do we learn to grow and become strong and resolved.

In this book, we will explore the feminine path to finding your life purpose, or as I call it, "the G-spot of your soul".

Though you will read a lot about sexuality in these pages, please know that this is NOT a book about sex. Our sexuality is our connection with the world and with others; it is bigger than the sexual act itself. **When we, as women, connect with our inner purpose, we, in a sense, make love to everything and everyone around us.** We transcend the physical realm and enter the world of the spirit. Sexual energy is like dynamite for our subsconsious mind--it opens us up. When we talk about sex in this book we're not referring to some basic animal urge. We are talking about a state of transcendence in your soul as you discover your soul's g-spot--when your entire body, your physical, emotional, mental, astral, etheric, celestial and casual selves – become one unified source of pleasure and power. Finding your life purpose by using your sexual energy allows you to experience a temporary death in the physical realm, and, through this experience you will realize your own immortality.

To live your life and devour it- means to become even more "alive". Becoming more alive means to develop and grow. Therefore, sexual energy is the way of increasing human pleasure and growth.

Are you ready to start your journey?

This path will unfold in front of you – so be patient as I know you've gotten used to getting your wishes fulfilled by striving or banging your head off many walls.

❖ In Chapter 2 we will discuss our **spiritual makeup** and understand **the importance of finding our purpose.** Unfortunately, in our society we talk at great length about making money and being pretty but so little about soul, we are not taught how to align our thoughts, listen and nurture our soul - how to follow our inner call, how to trust our emotions and instincts- which is the medium of communication with our inner divine. But finding the G-spot- that sweet spot that makes us happy, ecstatic, passionate in life should be our #1 need and goal.

❖ In Chapter 3 we will discuss **how to live your life the "feminine way".** We are taught to be goal-oriented, to choose one focus and stick to it. People who have multiple passions and interests, who change their jobs or jump from one field to another are frowned upon as non-serious or untrustworthy. But the real joy and pleasure in life (and sex) come from the experimenting and focusing on the process, not the result.

❖ In Chapter 4 we will talk **about the necessity of going through different experiences in life and trying on different**

roles before finding that "sweet spot" of yours. Like the sexual G-spot, it is not easy to find our life's purpose right away. It takes trial and error and experimentation. Some of which are negative and very destructive. Yes, we will be talking about our sadomasochistic tendencies as they apply not only to the bedroom, but mainly to our search of our place in this world.

❖ In Chapter 5 we will talk about **the importance of pain**. Like the G-spot, sometimes finding your life purpose is a painful experience but all worth it in the end. In our society we are practicing positive attitudes, we are taught to say affirmations and smile and say we are fine and Ok to the question "How are you?" We are not supposed to show negative emotions as they are considered a sign of weakness. As we grow up, we are ashamed of feeling down. If we are uncomfortable we feel paranoid. We seek medicine if we are out of sync with life. We are not apt at dealing with changes as *"life-changing experiences"* are considered to be near-death experiences, catastrophic events that change our perceptions of life - and are thus avoided by all means. We are so driven by the comfort that we are keeping our soul (like our bodies) out of shape and lethargic.

❖ Chapter 6 will unfold **the path of finding the true G-spot of your soul.** You will learn that it is NOT a comfortable or easy experience as one would like it to be, and will construct your own understanding of your souls' purpose.

❖ Chapter 7 will help you get **into the consistent mode of creating multi-orgasmic living** and will warn you about some downfalls you might experience during this process.

DR. MARINA KOSTINA

As you read this book, remind yourself that without pain, we cannot experience joy.

As a society, we are hardwired to sit on our tush in a comfortable lethargic state. I invite you to start EXPERIENCING life, rather than just observing it, getting used to the uncomfortable and finding the deepest inspirations in your pain.

We grow from the dark much more and faster than we do from the light and often our deepest gifts (and the source of our passion, pleasure and joy) are located where it hurts the most. Life purpose is a waltz between pain, pleasure, play and power and in that intersection we find our Gspot - the true Gspot of our Soul, as the *"real beauty lies in whatever that hurts."*

For me, all my trials and tribulations resulted in the most incredible outcome- finding my life purpose and aligning my entire life around it. Once I did that my business took off, my lifestyle changed and, most importantly, I started living a passionate and joyful life. I started TRULY trusting myself. While before I outsourced my reasons for happiness outside of myself to online courses that promised to give me love overnight or make me rich in a click of a button, to gurus that were telling me how to live my life and lead my business, to magical objects and juju. Now I use these means as supplementary help, not as my guide as I have found my own internal compass that is never wrong and is ALWAYS working for me. I hope that this book will open your path to your internal compass. You might have heard many things I talk about here but try not to resist the *"old information"* maybe this time around it will provoke another emotion in you and inspire you to really enjoy your life.

Chapter 2: How Do You REALLY Look Naked?

"Beauty begins the moment you decide to be yourself."

-Coco Chanel

~ Goddess Freya~

Goddess Freya (as I call this client of mine for her struggle with her sexuality and her fierce personality) was a beautiful TV star with a hair of a lioness and a body of a goddess. I often watched her interviews and was wondering how nature can create such perfection- a perfect hourglass figure, a naturally blond hair- she was anyone's dream come true. When she came to me I was in shock.

Here, in the seclusion of our candle lit room, she showed me a side of her that no one has ever seen. Her glamour and her power went out the window… she was broken, depressed and miserable. She confessed that all her life she has been attracting abusive partners and has suffered from anxiety, insomnia, depression and bulimia. You see, exactly those qualities that I found beautiful and attractive in her, she despised.

Her hour-glass shaped figure was "fat" and "disproportionate", her gorgeous hair a haystack, the list goes on and on. She admitted that she could never look at herself naked and was always covered under blankets while making love to her partners. I realized then that the guys she was attracting were reflections of how she saw herself, not the objective reality.

We, women, tend to be the worst critics of our own body. So if you feel bad about your legs, belly, breasts, arms — I hear you. I was there too and so are millions of other women. Unfortunately, it is a normal feeling for us females.

It is interesting how our relationships with our bodies dictate our relationships with the partners and with the world. When we feel fit and sexy we are on top of the world and one with the world; but when our bodies feel unattractive to us we often create discord alienation and push partners, jobs, and opportunities away.

So how do you see yourself, honestly? Well, if you try to access this knowledge with your conscious mind you might fool yourself. Especially right after reading the paragraphs above. Your mind might want to create an illusion for you to be trapped in. Let's get into your subconscious mind. We are going to do a quick test that will show you exactly how you see yourself right now.

Ready? Let's go!

Close your eyes, start breathing slowly, take a full five breaths inhaling and exhaling slowly. Now look deep into your soul and imagine the staircase. What shape does it have? What material is it made of? What color is it? How many steps does it have?

Step 2:- Now quickly without thinking, place yourself on the staircase. Imagine yourself on this staircase and see which step are you on? Are you at the top? Near the bottom? Somewhere in the middle?

Step 3:- When you really see your position on the staircase, quickly place three important people for you on these stairs (your partner, or ex, your kids, your parents, etc...).

Try and interpret your results on the basis of your vision. See, the whole purpose of this technique is to reveal how you see yourself and how you see others in relation to you. The steps on the stairs correspond to the vibrations of your soul. The lower your placement on the staircase, the lower your vibrations. Being anywhere other than the top step indicates a missing link. Are others above you, below you, or at the same level as you? Your position or vibration is pivotal in manifesting a life of fulfillment, joy, and peace. Chances are if you found yourself on the lower steps you also do not live the life of your dreams and feel like you still have not found your life purpose or your true calling; since life purpose and self-love are inter-related concepts.

It is extremely difficult to have a high self-esteem and self-worth if you are not fulfilling your mission in life. On the contrary, if you know why you are here; if your life has a greater meaning and higher purpose, all enemies of self-esteem such as doubt, fear, self-criticism become mitigating. Even your not-so-perfect body (according to you) cannot interfere with your sense of fulfillment and joy that only living your passion and purpose can bring.

When you live your life on a mission nothing can stop you and stand in your way… not even yourself!

Your sense of self-esteem, joy and meaning comes from living an inspired life, and as one of my favorite authors Wayne Dyer always stated, the word *inspired* comes from two words: *in spirit*. It is time we get to the main point of this chapter- how do you REALLY look naked?

How Do You REALLY Look Naked?

You have more than one magnificent body. The physical body you are so familiar with isn't your only one. Located around it is your *energetic body*. Most of us can't see it, but the energetic body consists of several layers. These layers form an egg-shaped sphere, called the *aura*, which performs essential life functions. Everything is energy and energy creates vibrations. All things, people, and events have their vibrations. You create experiences in life based on the vibrational match you have with others. If your vibrations are low - you attract people, circumstances, and situations that are "low" or "negative" as we believe them to be.

On the other hand, if your vibrations are high, you will attract positive people favorable for your vibes. What we perceive as our physical material world, is not physical or material at all, in fact, it is far from it. This has been proven by many including Nobel Prize winning physicists and scientists. For instance, Niels Bohr, a

Danish physicist, observed, *"If quantum mechanics hasn't profoundly shocked you, you haven't understood it yet. Everything we call real is made of things that cannot be regarded as real."* Quantum physicists discovered that we consist of energy and vibration.

You are still not convinced, right? Ok, let's continue…

Have you ever walked into your house where you partner or roommate lives and right away felt a sickness and heaviness in your stomach? You have not even said "hi" yet or seen the person, but you already know that they are not in a good mood? Well, that is their *'aura'*, their vibes, their energetic field are hissing at you.

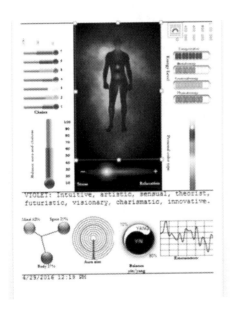

Picture 1: An energetic Field of a Human

Above is the picture from one of my energy analysis sessions of a real person, shown through my biofeedback machine (a machine that reads one's energy and transfers it onto a computer screen). The colors around the person are her aura or *"character overtones"*. Since ancient times we have seen similar pictures and paintings of different spiritual leaders across various traditions, but one striking aspect common among all of them is the halo that surrounds their head and their bodies, known as the Aura- energy field. This aura represents your physical, mental, emotional as well as spiritual energies. It is often seen as a mix of fine colored frequencies where each color defines its nature and characteristics. Each "type" of aura has its unique character features, missions, motivations, talents, obstacles and life purposes.

Now scientific research shows that the aura is an electromagnetic field of energy that extends all around our body for about four tofive feet in an average healthy body and appears to be depleted in cases of an unhealthy person. The aura of a person is directly connected to their level of health in regards to their physical vitality, mental clarity, emotional well-being as well as highly positive spiritual energies. So a person who is healthy at all these levels has a bigger and brighter aura and vice versa in the case of an unhealthy person.

Compare the two pictures below. The picture of the aura of the person on the left is bigger, brighter and more concrete. While the picture to the right seems to be blighted by affliction. The picture to the left is of a spiritual practitioner- no wonder why his aura is so healthy. While the picture to the right represents a person who has been addicted to drugs and alcohol, their aura is smaller, darker and has "holes" in them and in some areas touches his body.

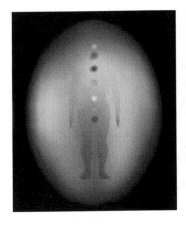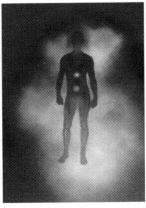

Picture 2: Aura comparison between a healer and a drug addict

In a nutshell, the aura is an energy field that primarily serves two purposes:-

❖ **It is our presence:** - The way others perceive us and form an opinion on us. You probably noticed that some people you meet might not be considered attractive by social standards, but you feel such warmth and adoration from the second you meet them. While other *"socially attractive"* people just cause a very strong repulsive feeling in you... that is because *you are feeling their aura!*

❖ **It protects us:** - Our aura helps to ward off unwanted events/ people/ circumstances. Ideally, your aura should be a solid oval, if the oval has indentations or holes, it is weakened. The closer the aura comes to the body the more prone we are to the physical manifestation of pain, sickness or disease. If the aura has holes in it, we drain energy and feel fatigued; and keep attracting so-called *"energetic vampires"* who like to 'suck' our energy through these holes.

How Do We Create Our Reality?

Scientists and researchers all around the globe have a general consensus that the solid looking matter is made up of pure energy which is vibrating at a specific frequency and gives it special properties, such as shape, size, texture, etc... Remember your physics lesson in 9th grade, in which you studied that solid matter is composed of atoms that are tightly packed together and exhibit vibrational motion and these vibrations are caused by subatomic energy possessing particles, which are protons, electrons and neutrons. So when these particles vibrate in their nucleus, a small electrical impulse is generated in our body and according to the famous law of physics *"When there is an electrical field around a body, a magnetic field gets developed automatically"*.

So the tiny electrical impulses in our body result in the formation of a magnetic field around our body which is known as the aura (aka electromagnetic field of the body). Since everything in this universe is made up of the same constituent particles - electrons, protons, neutrons, etc..., we can deduce that everything has an aura and everything has vibrations. ***Low vibrations attract lower vibrating people, events, and circumstances. High vibrations attract higher vibrating entities into one's life***. Remember our beautiful Goddess Freya? No matter how gorgeous she was on the outside it is her inside vibration that attracted those abusive relationships in her life.

Are you still not convinced?

Have you ever seen how a guitar is tuned? When you place your finger on the string and strike it, another string that is of the same vibration starts moving in unison on its own! That is because each of the strings has the same frequency.

You are that string! You bring into your reality things, events and people that are on the same frequency as you!

If we study ancient Indian texts, especially the yoga sutras, we will come to know about the chakra system, an important aspect of our Aura. So depending on the health and balance of our chakras, we create (or prevent) the flow of positive or negative into our lives. Let's very briefly see how each chakra contributes to different aspects of your life.

1st Chakra: (tailbone location) It represents our foundation, our feeling of being grounded, and our contact with the Mother Earth. It is also the center of manifesting things in the material world. Your 1st chakra is out of balance if you feel broke, financially insecure, and unable to achieve goals or move forward, or if you have issues with the immune system, obesity, anorexia nervosa, knees, hips, legs, lower back and sexual organs. Fear, rape, and abortion block 1st Chakra. Balancing and opening it up is vital to your sense of stability, financial abundance, and health in this world. This chakra is also super important for the maintenance of your life purpose once you find it.

2nd Chakra: (2 inches below your belly button) This chakra represents our connection to our sexuality, creativity, and intuition. Your chakra needs healing if you block the sense of abundance, pleasure, sexuality, creativity, and *"goddessness"* or if you have problems with kidneys, a stiff lower back, constipation, muscle spasms, bloated belly, infertility, kidneys, bladder, and the large intestine. The unresolved feeling of guilt usually blocks this chakra.

3rd Chakra: (Your Solar Plexus) 3rd chakra represents our ability to be confident and in control of our lives. It is our center of personal power, the place of ego, passions, impulses, anger, and strength. Your chakra is out of alignment if you experience digestive difficulties, liver problems, diabetes, nervous exhaustion, and food allergies. The body parts for this chakra include the stomach, liver, gallbladder, pancreas, and the small intestine. Shame usually blocks this chakra.

4th Chakra (heart): This chakra is the center of compassion, empathy and the ability to give and receive love. It also connects the body and mind with spirit. The heart chakra is unbalanced if people experience a heart attack, high blood pressure, insomnia, and difficulty in breathing. Body parts for the fourth chakra include the heart, lungs, circulatory system, shoulders, and upper back. Grief, resentment or remorse block this chakra.

5th Chakra: (throat) This chakra represents your ability to communicate your truth and your authentic self; it's the center of sound, and expression of creativity via thought, speech, and writing. It is also the location of the possibility for change, transformation and healing. The unbalanced 5th chakra is manifested in the hyperthyroid, skin irritations, ear infections, sore throat, inflammations, and back pain. Body parts for the fifth chakra are throat, neck, teeth, ears, and thyroid gland. Lies that we tell ourselves usually block this chakra.

6th Chakra: (third eye) This chakra represents your ability to focus on, and see the big picture, to have intuition and imagination, to feel oneness with everything. It is also the center of psychic ability and higher intuition. If you are unbalanced in this center, you are probably experiencing headaches, insomnia, blurred vision, blindness, and eyestrain. Body parts for this chakra include the eyes, face, brain, lymphatic and endocrine system.

7th Chakra: (crown) This chakra represents our ability to be fully connected spiritually; it's the center of enlightenment, dynamic thought, and energy. It is unbalanced if you experience migraines, headaches and depression.

While all seven chakras are important for having a balanced life and finding and supporting your life purpose, the 2nd chakra is the place of your feminine power where you should focus your attention and nourishment in order to tune in to the '*flow*'. Interestingly enough that this chakra is located in our belly and is responsible for our feeling of sexiness. Yet it is also a center of creativity and manifestation. Thus, our feeling of *"sexiness"* is directly connected to our creativity, life purpose and…. Spirituality. Yes, creative, sexual, and spiritual energies are the same!

The Center Of Your Power

Of all chakras, the 2nd one is the center of your pleasure, creativity, play and purpose. It is the sure way to feel your goddessness. It is the center of your power because when we drop into this space and use all the tools that this chakra gives us, we get into this different plane, where our creative faculties levitate to a higher level and when we reach that state of being, we encounter no problems, no sense of separation, pain or doubt. We also are aligned with our purpose here.

Most women, however, have blocked or destabilized their 2nd chakra causing separation from their sexuality, creativity and spirituality. The main reason for this is GUILT that we, women, are so familiar with.

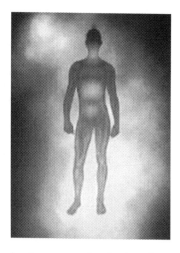

Look at the picture of one of my clients. Do you see how fuzzy and small their 2nd chakra (orange) is? This person carries a lot of guilt in her. This guilt stems from childhood and was connected to an event that no longer seems significant. Because of the unresolved nature of the emotion, this guilt has been affecting the person for over 20 years! At the time of our session, this client did not feel sexy, had gynaecological pain and did not have a sexual relationship with her husband for over a year. Once she opened this center, not only her relationships with her husband improved but she changed her profession and started her own business. So we just learned that guilt blocks the 2nd chakra. *How ironic is that many mothers carry guilt here while this chakra is also the center of fertility?*

So now you know how you REALLY look naked. That your self-image and the flow (or stagnation) in your life depend on your vibrational state and the condition of your aura. Do you want to feel great naked? Then you need to learn your vibes and raise them. How do you do this, you may ask? You can, of course, use lots of "outside" help- attend yoga classes, do reiki and other energy healing sessions, but there are three things you can do for yourself. These three miracle tools are: pleasure, creativity and play.

Pleasure

The 2nd chakra's best healing is... pleasure. Unfortunately, nowadays, pleasure is a facet that is almost forbidden for women. We are taught to suppress the need for pleasure and thus cut ourselves from the biggest source of our strength. Yes, pleasure is the surest way to fill your tanks quickly and connect with your life purpose. Remember, society teaches you to achieve, compete, and push. We label ourselves "successful" when we overcome many issues to achieve our new position, promotion etc... With our willpower, we can, of course, reach our desired goals but the second we relax, life will slam its door shut on us. Have you ever gotten that new promotion only to learn in a few months that the company has been dissolved?

Your biggest strength as a woman is a state of pleasure. Think, what really brings pleasure to you (and by pleasure I don't mean just sexual pleasure)? However, your sexuality is a huge part of your overall pleasure in life and your identity. Yes, often we hide or are even embarrassed of that side of ourselves, yet it is sexuality that makes us true goddesses. In ancient mythology of various cultures we see that gods had pretty orgasmic lives. Yet they did not want humans to be like them and they hid the knowledge of sex from the humans. Some researchers interpret the myth of the Prometheus exactly this way. The fire that Prometheus brought was the knowledge of sex and gods punished him for that as knowledge of sexuality has made a god out of a man.

We can also see how in tantric tradition the only way to be free from a desire is to submit to it. All desires are focused and are used for the awakening of kundalini, a snake fire. Thus we can see that sex- is life, sex is existence and creation. A person can only be completely free and happy if he/she has enough energy to manifest his/her life. Sexuality will be used and the energy will be awakened. It is a difficult journey but the price is worth it. A human must reach the deepest darkness of the abyss in order to awaken a sleeping dragon, to awaken him and make him fly. A person must find his sexuality, awaken it and reach the state of "goddessness" and happiness.

Homework: - Make a list of at least 2-3 things and try to do them at minimum several times a week, see the effect they have on you. Do they bring something positive or spark a welcome change? Keep embracing these pleasure practices and incorporate them into your daily habits of self-empowerment.

Creativity

When we get to the realm of creativity, we are instantly out of our mind and we are able to connect with something bigger than ourselves, our divine, God, or whatever name you have for that force; and it is not by chance that *'creativity'* and the *Creator*, and *procreation* come from the same root—they are all located here, in the 2nd Chakra!

See, in the creative arts, there is no "wrong" or "right". It is impossible to make mistakes in art, as it is all about expressing yourself through a medium. When you learn how to express yourself authentically your self-doubts and insecurities will start disappearing, as nothing will seem to be "wrong" anymore with how you look, act or feel (just like in art!). Do you see how when you expand your 2nd chakra and become more creative your self-esteem also expands? You also transcend the duality of good vs bad, right and wrong and start experiencing oneness. And from this state, it is much easier to access your life purpose.

Homework: - Set time for creative projects at least once a week. Don't be attached by the results, enjoy the process, even if it means to knit and undo the entire piece to start over, or cook and give your creation away to pigeons, or paint over the same canvas. While regularly engaging in creative tasks you are teaching your psyche about how to access the realm of the unknown and bring those elements into the material world, i.e. you are learning the art of manifestation.

Play

It is sad to assert that majority of my clients do not have joy or a sense of fulfillment in their lives, they are merely drudging on with life. Funny, how joy is one of the highest vibrations out there! According to Dr. Hawkins, the creator of the scale of consciousness where each emotion has a corresponding vibration, joy has a vibration of 540 MHz which is even higher than LOVE (500MHz)! When we play, we become connected to our inner child- the source of true joy. Through play, we can really understand what our calling is, what makes our soul sing, laugh, and dance—we can almost touch that invisible energy that surrounds every one of us.

Homework: - Write down what makes you excited, playful and stirs your imagination. If you are completely disconnected from your joy, try to remember what games you used to play as a child. List them- recreate the memory and try to feel the exuberance and innocence of your childhood. How can you re-create this feeling in your life now? If you have little children follow them and participate in their games. See how easy and fun their life is, how in the flow they are.

Remember, you cannot be in joy and out of the flow... Therefore enjoying life should be our #1 priority. Get rid of all guilt that you created around the concept of having fun!

When you incorporate these three tools into your life, you are going to start the process of expansion and will raise your vibration dramatically. For those who want to deepen their practices, I will offer three more powerful exercises I use with my clients. These are: *"fire your inner critique exercise"*, *"matreshka technique"* and *"daily mantra for expansion"*

Exercise 1: Fire Your Inner Critic

Before we expand your 2nd chakra we need to get rid of the stuff that is blocking you from getting there. As I already mentioned, guilt blocks most women and disconnects them from their goddessness. By the way, once your 2nd chakra is open and flowing you will even experience better orgasms and start creating things you have never even dreamed off.

Remember, that guilt manifests itself in the nasty inner critic. No one, not even your worst enemy is as dangerous to you as your inner critic. This little sucker that sits inside of your brain is hell-bent to disconnect you from your life purpose. It is his main agenda to keep you away from your power, your talents, and your brilliance so you can serve him and be his slave. Now, if we use its own methods (aka bullying, pushing against, resisting and resenting), we are going to lose. I mean, he has forever to learn the skills of killing your soul. So we are going to have to use another approach. We are going to embrace it and show it who the Daddy is (I mean, the Mommy!). So we are going to use the following activity that I call, "*Fire your inner critic*" technique. In reality, we are not going to fire it entirely (we don't want to have a disgruntled ex-employee planning how to burn us down, right?) we are going to assign it a new job! So for this activity, you need to take a piece of paper, and write the following: -

I (first and last name), today, (date), announce that the vacancy for the Inner Critic in my life is closed. All employees occupying this position are immediately dismissed and fired. I no longer need their services.

Date: -

Signature:

Put the paper away. After some time, it will help you recollect who criticized you and how their criticism turned into your inner critic. You can start adding your own self-debilitating thoughts and add them to your announcement above. This will be your first step. The Universe will start bringing people who support your life mission and purpose and help you heal your inner critic.

Exercise 2: The Matryoshka Technique

Now that we have calmed your inner critic, you have created some space for your soul to thrive, but in order to connect with something bigger than yourself, you need to create a big space!

Remember the Russian nesting dolls, where one doll is inside the other? They are called Matryoshka. Our conscious and subconscious mind have a similar structure. The Matryoshka technique is based on the idea that just like it is impossible to move from the smallest Matryoshka doll to the largest one, it is also impossible to jump from the state of scarcity to the state of abundance right away (that is why affirmations often do not work. You can sit for hours telling yourself you are a millionaire, but if you feel poor inside, nothing is going to change). The trick is to get to the point of abundance gradually (one Matreshka at a time). At each new belief stop and notice: does it feel comfortable or do you have resistance inside? If you have resistance, create a smaller step between your ideas. Consider the following example: -

Current state: - I feel broke. I charge 30 dollars an hour.

Desired State: - I charge 500 dollars an hour.

Now, this idea is TOO scary and not real to me; I feel resistance. So I need to create a series of beliefs that take me from my current state to my desired state. I will test each belief for resistance (if resistance is present, I will come up with an extra step):

Step 1 (START): I feel broke. I am charging 30 dollars an hour

Step 2: I can charge more than I charge now (Checkpoint: Does this feel good? Do you believe this statement?)

Step 3: Any resistance is a belief that can be changed (Checkpoint: Does this feel good? Do you believe this statement?)

Step 4: Premium prices can transform my life (Checkpoint: Does this feel good? Do you believe this statement?)

Step 5: You can charge premium prices and feel authentic in all areas of your business (Checkpoint: Does this feel good? Do you believe this statement?)

Step 6: I can charge premium prices and still feel authentic in all areas of my business (Checkpoint: Does this feel good? Do you believe this statement?)

Step 7 (GOAL): I can charge $500/ hour without *"selling my soul"* (Checkpoint: Does this feel good? Do you believe this statement?)

Remember, each step needs to feel comfortable and safe, with no resistance inside. Now make your own "Matreshka path" to your desired states (add or delete any steps to match YOUR internal resistance).

Exercise 3: Your Daily Mantra

Your beliefs have a lot of power and we are going to voice this mantra every day looking at our reflection in the mirror, feeling with each cell the truth of these words and change our subconscious self-limiting beliefs. So looking at yourself in the mirror say the following:

"I believe that you are a genius woman, a muse. You inspire others to bring your wants in your life. You create everything with ease and grace and communicate with others with curiosity and respect. Your life is euphoric, pleasurable and comfortable. You learn so much

from others and through this practice you learn about yourself, loving yourself more and more. You communicate intelligently and elegantly with others. People around you are craving to be near you because during this communication, they feel inspired and good about themselves, which in turn raises their self-value. They love, respect and adore you for this. You are a source of harmony and peace. You are successfully attracting and bringing into your life all of your heart's desires. When you desire and receive – you expand!"

Chapter 3: Don't Lose Your Yin in His Yang

"I think of masculine and feminine energy like two sides to a battery. There is a plus side and a minus side, and in order to make something turn on, you need to have opposites touching..."

-Tracy McMillan

~ *Goddess Aphrodite* ~

Goddess Aphrodite, a gorgeous client of mine in her early 40s (long dark hair, olive skin, almond-shaped eyes)—a total stunner, a mother of 3, a successful business owner was sitting in front of me crying, shrugging her shoulders and feeling small... Anyone who saw her would not even guess how low she felt aboutherself... most women would want to have her curvy sexy body, her full hair and confident look, men would totally call her a 10... yet she felt like a complete failure, a 1, or even a 0....

At her age, she has already been married and divorced three times. She said that every next marriage she purposefully chose a different type of man so she would not make the same mistakes. Yet all of them ended up in failure, aka divorce. I asked her to describe her marriages and men to me. The first husband of the Goddess Aphrodite was a very weak man according to her. She quickly lost all respect for him and left him. The second one was an abuser who used to beat her up and have violent arguments with her. The third one was a cheater...

She could not understand what was wrong as through all her relationships she was a giver, she took care of her men and loved them, doing a lot of things around the house, serving them while also running a business. She put everyone first and forgot herself- how ungrateful were all these men!

With each marriage, her joy for love shrunk and her business was less successful and was losing money. Orgasms... what orgasms?? The last marriage had her dry and cold... with no sex for over 2 years... Now she was a complete mess... a loser and with no purpose (other than her kids of course) in her life!

I looked at her with joy. 'It is great!", I said as she looked at me with the eyes full of surprise. "These three men are perfect teachers that show you three possible scenarios of emasculation of a man".

When we, women, mainly live from our masculine energy—a man has three options:

a. he either shrinks (her first hubby)

b. pushes back (second hubby)

c. leaves us for others (her third hubby)

This happens when we occupy all the masculine space in the relationship. (Please note, I don't justify abuse or cheating. But I want to show you how our energies attract these people into our lives- remember from Chapter 2- we are all energy).

When women live predominantly in the male energy, they disconnect from their female source- the source of pleasure, joy, creativity and sensuality, and thus, automatically disconnect from their purpose- where their sexuality and orgasmic living is located!

While we can still make a successful "CAREER" with our masculine energy it is almost impossible to find our true soul purpose without connecting to our feminine source of power.

The reason why our Goddess Aphrodite has been hiding her "light" is because her entire life she'd been focused ONLY on her accomplishments, on the outcomes, on the results. She believed that she could ONLY be loved for what she DID. And so she pushed, and over functioned, and emasculated her men, slowly blurring her light more and more with each relationship....

My client's story is a typical story for many females. We lose our light and our purpose in a constant chase after being loved FOR something. We over function and run ourselves on empty in order to be good wives, moms, daughters, and citizens. In this drained condition, we cannot connect to our light and thus fulfil the purpose of our soul. Neither can we connect with our sexuality, sensuality, or experience orgasms. You, see it is all connected! Our soul (and our bodies) in return keep reminding us of why we came to this world... and when we don't listen, it keeps creating circumstances (such as failed relationships, sickness, etc...) that make us wake up to our purpose.

Sometimes we need to be hit with a frying pan by the Universe sort of speaking to start looking into our soul and finding the light within.

While that is one way of connecting with your inner soul, let's try a more pleasant way- connecting through our femininity.

So what is feminine energy?

The Tale Of Oxytocin And Testosterone

In many cultures, we can encounter folkloric female figures, such as Russian rusalki (mermaids) or Greek sirens, the fierce female spirits that have the power over men. Russian rusalki, for instance, lure men into the depth of the forest with their beautiful voices and naked bodies and then tickle them to death or give them tools to succeed in life (depending on how these men behave).

Greek sirens live on a beautiful island surrounded by water. They sing their captivating songs which enchant men who are passing by on the boats. The men cannot help themselves but keep on listening to the hypnotic sounds of the sirens, they cross oceans and are willing to face the death and break their boats off the shore of the island only to have a glimpse of these beauties, only to hear their song... These creatures are the most enchanting and powerful indeed. We all can learn from them, so let's look at them at a detail...

These females don't go around seeking men, they don't stand on the shore waving at them or calling them... they are not sad if the boats are not approaching their island. They laugh and play and create with their fellow female spirits. They enjoy their beauty and nakedness (and for sure they are not putting themselves down because of the extra pounds). They are so connected to their core, to who they are, to their authentic self that their song becomes the most enigmatic to those who hear it... And so is YOUR song when you connect with it – it has the power to make you the most attractive, beautiful female despite all your so-called shortcomings!

When we don't express the song that we came to this world to sing we are committing energetic suicide- we energetically cut off the flow of our higher chakras – intuition and spiritual guidance—from the rest of our lives…And thus we energetically hang ourselves. Look at this picture that shows the blocked 5th chakra- the center of our authentic power and self-expression—do you see how fuzzy it is and how it cuts the flow of the higher chakras to the lower ones (see how bleak the lower chakras are like they need more food, more life)?

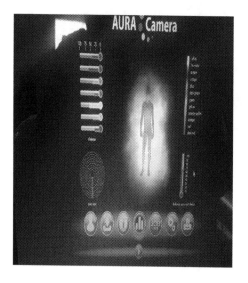

Pic 4: Imbalanced chakras

Therefore, like the sirens, the main purpose and attraction power of the woman is not in her "doing', but in her "being", in the realization of her perfection as her birthright. By the way, in the ancient Sanskrit, the word "woman" means "perfect".

So understand that you are already perfect and all you need is to learn how to relax into that perfection and exude it to the world.

According to Chinese philosophy, two main energies rule this world: yang (male) and yin (female). These forces are seemingly opposite yet together they create an interconnected, interdependent wholesome union where each complements the other. In our relationships, we are supposed to value these differences, accept them and welcome them. Did you notice the choice of words I used above? Interdependent, interconnected…. However, we are usually so good at being independent—which implies separation, and so bad at creating true interdependence- which requires understanding and respecting the differences and opposite forces.

We all know the two hormones in the body that drive us, the oxytocin and the testosterone. And if you didn't know, now you know. *Testosterone* is the male hormone, responsible for setting goals, achieving, and doing things. This is our Yang, male energy. While *oxytocin* is the female energy (Yin) that makes us happy and relaxed. To successfully function in life and relationships we need both, and if you want to have a harmonious relationship you need to always strive for the Yang-Yin balance.

But the sad thing is, many women have now lost their oxytocin - their female energy, instead, they're now full of testosterone - male energy, and that shows up in their lives in different destructive ways. By the way, women who function from their female energy predominately are usually never alone because they don't occupy the space of the male energy. But women who have a vast amount of male energy, often find themselves not happy and single. Why? Because they can't attract a partner as they emit their male vibes to the Universe. It is the same of homosexual and transsexual relationships as female energy does not necessarily mean "woman" and masculine energy does not necessarily mean "men". We are talking about the balance of the two, the dance between them.

In this chapter, I want you to start discovering the beauty of each. Recognize that despite your pretty looks you are most probably living mainly from your *"male"* source and it is time to enhance your own female Yin energy. It will attract partnerships, abundance, passion, and creativity, and connect you to your life purpose with ease and grace (as opposed to by pushing, competing, and striving).

The Yang Or The Sun Energy

Sorry to break it to you but if you are reading this book you are most probably using the Yang, the Sun energy in your life. Often women believe that the true female energy lies in the fullness of their breasts, the length of their legs and the size of their waist. NOT EVEN CLOSE! (By the way, in my research, men have stated that the most attractive physical feature of a woman is her...butt, followed by her eyes and her smile).

But BESIDES these physical characteristics the MOST attractive features of the woman according to my research on men are kindness, loyalty, passion for life and acceptance of self. Now, these are qualities of the MOON energy or YIN; and these are the qualities of a woman that are connected to her purpose.

You see, the society tells us that the goal of a woman is to *serve*- our kids, our parents, and our men. But while we take care of everyone around us, we don't take care of ourselves. The thing is, serving is an action of *leaning forward*. Women and men have different energetic centers of power and thus the direction of "leaning" is also different for each of them. For men, their energetic center is their head. They lead with *the head*. They conquer, achieve, compete, and… SERVE…. All these actions (including serving!) are directed at DOING and "leaning forward." Just close your eyes and imagine these actions in your mind. You will see that you are moving forward. RIGHT? Now let's see what the feminine energy looks and feels like.

The Yin Or The Moon Energy

For women, *the lower belly and the womb area* is the female center, as we already discussed in chapter 2. The feminine energy invites us to accept, preserve, relax, and just BE—i.e., to "lean back." When a woman leans back she welcomes life and things, people and circumstances come TO HER, as opposed to her running after them (just like the sirens!).

Why is this important? Remember the old saying, "Happy wife - Happy life"? And why? The world needs the Moon energy - a woman's energy for times of crisis. During hard times - the calm woman saves the situation.

But the woman can have enough MOON energy in the times of crisis ONLY if in the times of peace she takes care of herself and generates, relishes and expands her female forces (i.e. "leans back!").

Unfortunately, we do the opposite- we forget to take care of ourselves, we give, give, give and run on empty. We over function and get resentful. We cook and clean and wait for the man to come home and notice our hard work, but he doesn't. Why? Is it because he is a jerk? Nope, my dear. Most of the times (with a few exceptions) men FEEL your overfunctioning energy, you're leaning forward, your male, exhausted, running on empty vibes. They don't need your soup or your clean floors. They NEED YOUR FEMININE, RELAXED, PEACEFUL ENERGY. When you lean back, you create space for him to show up as your hero, as your provider, as your protector, as your supporter (roles, by the way, that are most desired by men according to my research!). So next time you feel like you have to cook a dinner and do it running on empty, stop yourself and ask your man to order in. He will be much happier to do it than to experience your masculine, deprived and exhausted energy. When the man feels like your hero, he wants to serve YOU. When you learn how to accept this, you can lean back, feel gratitude and your femininity, feel full, sexy, sensual, and desired. You feel like a true goddess! This is the state from which you can connect to your passion and your purpose in life.

So, my dear ladies, you have a responsibility in this world- to preserve your moon energy. Which means that you need to become a bit more SELFISH; and that is a most selfless act.

Everybody's mood depends on the woman's after all. So, keep your happiness level high. Make yourself happy. And don't put that responsibility on a man. He is NOT here to fill you with joy. YOU ARE.

Let this be your mantra: *My goal is to receive, accept, and preserve my moon energy.*

So, you might ask, how can you increase your moon energy? Here are things that can help you in this process:

Tools To Fill Your Moon Energy

a. Learn to lean back, relax and enjoy (vs push forward and strive)

This will be the best homework ever, my beauties. As I encourage you to stop over-functioning and worrying about everyone else in life but to lean back, relax and enjoy yourselves and your lives. Connecting to your feminine power does not mean losing control. It actually empowers you as it shifts the focus on YOU, making YOU the creator of your experience and emphasizes the importance of your energy.

Feminine energy (leaning back, being, accepting and thanking) is a powerful approach to getting ANYTHING into your life-relationships, happiness AND your purpose.

Look at the fairytales- the prince needs to swim through the river, kill the dragon, climb the tower, and get to the Moon and back to get to his princess. The princess is NOT sitting at the window screaming at her prince, why he is taking so long... or offers him a "better" tool to kill the dragon, or, even better, jumps on the horse herself "because he is taking too long... She sends the request to her man, trusts that he will fulfill it and while he is doing all of those deeds she is enjoying herself- playing with other princesses, brushing her hair, doing creative activities.... And as a result stays true to herself and receives her wish (the Moon, the love, the prince, etc).

Now, some of you might see it as being passive in life. I used to think so too... but I realized that whenever I actually had to push against something it ended up to be the wrong thing. Only when

I relaxed, found joy and let go of my obsession with the results, enjoying the process of what is... only then did I get a message, a revelation, a new opportunity, (or a prince!).

So the primary task of modern women (aka modern goddesses) is to understand what energetic frequency she vibrates as that is the frequency that creates our reality. How to quickly assess your vibration?

Look around: what do you see at this moment in your life in its different aspects? Your life is a direct indicator of the level of your energy vibration.

- What kind of people are you surrounded with?

- Do you like them or do they irritate you?

- Are you satisfied with the interior of the house where you live?

- Do you love your job? Your income?

- Do you enjoy your lifestyle?

Your outer life reflects your inner energetic vibration. Do you have an insultingly low salary, a soul-wrenching job, a disconnected, lazy man next to you? Yes-Yes, my dear! It's all a mere reflection of your vibration! It's a part of you-this man, this job, this level of income.....it is a reflection of YOUR energy. Instead of conquering, achieving, or attaining *"things"* you need to start FLOWING. Flow is when the *"right"* people, right amounts of money, right partners and right opportunities start opening up in front of you. The flow is also the only state where you can get to your true life purpose.

FIND THE G-SPOT OF YOUR SOUL

A woman in the flow is open for great things to happen in her life, she has the "space" inside of her and in her psyche that allows her to believe that she deserves such goods in life and she is full of gratitude when she receives them. A woman that has low vibration always tries to pay for something. Why does it happen? Because she does not believe she is WORTHY of great things in life and she also does not understand that she is energetically very strong.

Make a list of things that make you feel relaxed and joyful. Close your eyes, imagine, are you leaning forward or back when you are doing them? If you are leaning back- add them to your daily and weekly planner. In general, in each situation try to be aware of the direction of your leaning. Soon you will notice that in most situations of conflict, struggle and uncomfortable competition you are leaning forward. Stop, lean back, drop into your womb and from here feel what the course of action needs to be. Often just by shifting your energy, you shift the situation.

So your primary goal is to keep your energy, expand it and elevate it. Then and only then can you be connected to your life purpose. And once you are connected to your life purpose YOUR ENERGY KEEPS REPLENISHING AUTOMATICALLY because you become connected to the divine, to the universal energy. You become a channel of that energy; you start living in the flow.

What are some other ways to lean back? There are numerous ways to do it, but you can start at least with these:

1. Meditate and do spiritual practices such as yoga, tai-chi, reiki, etc...

2. Do creative activities (cooking- but ONLY from inspiration, not from obligation), painting, dancing, sculpting, knitting, etc. When we are creative, we are connected to the Creator, to the divine energy, and thus we replenish ourselves. When we are in creative mode, we are accessing our most precious talents and receive guidance for our life purpose

3. Be in your body (instead of your mind). No, seriously. The mind is where the problems are. You CANNOT FIND YOUR LIFE PURPOSE IN YOUR MIND. So take any opportunity to get out of it. One of the best things to do is to connect with a physical activity that takes you away from your mind. For each of us, it is a different activity—for someone, it is walking, for another person, it is yoga. For me, personally, when I do Zumba I cannot think much. The second I get distracted by some thought outside of the class, I lose the step! Find the activity that keeps you 100% in your body.

4. Connect with your girls. You have to make time to do girly things with your female friends.

5. Spoil yourself on a regular basis. No money? No problem. Do little things- like taking baths with candles, using Groupon for massages, a mani and pedi. Getting a diffuser and essential oils, etc...

6. Keep a diary of successes.

Another useful tool to activate your feminine energy is writing a daily diary of successes. You are going to resist it in the beginning (I did!) but the more you do it, the easier it will get. It does work! I and hundreds of my clients tried it and changed their internal limiting programs. So what is the diary of successes?

You buy a pretty (yes, it is a requirement!) notebook and you keep it next to your bed. Before going to bed you write down at least five accomplishments for the day. You list them not as a matter of fact, but RELATING to positive characteristics of yours. For example:

Wrong: I finally cleaned all the closets in my bedroom. *Right*: I cleaned all the closets in my bedroom because I am a tidy and organized person.

Sometimes you will be able to write tons of stuff there. Sometimes there is seemingly nothing to mention… The key here is not to judge the events. You need to train your brain to appreciate yourself even for small things, such as: "I put myself together and went to the meeting even though I was down and PMS-ing"… yes, this is a HUGE deal, so stop taking yourself for granted.

For this activity to be successful, you need to do it consistently every day. Remember, you are developing a new habit of seeing yourself in a positive light, of being your cheerleader, of concentrating on your power as opposed to a weakness. Usually, most of us negatively summarize our day, "I did not finish X, I screwed up X, etc..." When we are negative about ourselves we right away go into the masculine energy of protecting, defending, attacking striving and over functioning. When we feel good about ourselves we don't need to prove anything to anyone, we don't need to earn someone's love. We just ARE!

7. "The Ode to Me" Exercise

Tomorrow, after you just wake up (before your brain kicks in and starts giving you familiar negative talk) take a piece of paper and start writing 30-50 talents and positive qualities that you possess. YES!

Keep writing even if it sounds silly... whatever comes to mind- don't judge it. After you have written your talents, circle the "themes" that appear from the list. For example, ability to dance, the ability to make my house pretty, cool food presentation --- can go under the category of "creativity."

List top 3-5 categories you have.

Category #1: _____

Category #2: _____

Category #3: _____

Category #4: _____

Category #5: _____

These are your top five talents. What are some activities, jobs, businesses that you can use these talents for? These talents are insights for finding your life purpose. So keep this list as we will be using it in chapter 6!

8. Use two favorite male tools to expand your feminine powers.

Yes, many of us can learn from men who have two incredible qualities that we, women, usually are lacking and that can be the fastest road to our connection with life purpose.

First of all, most men are hedonists (from the Greek word hedone-pleasure). They like to do things that bring them pleasure and joy without an extra sense of guilt which we, women, like to add to any spoon of happiness we send into our mouth. By choosing pleasure and joy without fractioning yourself with the feelings of guilt, shame and obligation you maintain the wholesomeness of your being and expand your energy, which in turn brings you into the flow- a state where you find connection with your divine and the guidance for your life purpose. Remember, pleasure resides in your second chakra- the center of your power!

Second, most men live here and now. Their common inability to multitask is a blessing in disguise—they don't spread their energy in different directions at the same time. Like a woman can be at work and still keep thinking of her man, and her children and what she will be wearing on Friday night. Learning to focus on the present brings you into the now, into the state of "being", your Moon energy as we discussed above.

Hopefully, you start realizing by now the importance of using your feminine energy. Start accumulating feminine energy by following the steps listed above. Here is a little trick I use to get out of feeling guilty that most of us are conditioned to when focusing on our own happiness and ourselves.

Start seeing yourself as a CHANNEL through which the energy is sent to the world, to your kids, your parents, your partners. If you become a conductor of this energy and not THE SOURCE of it, you will realize that your #1 priority is to keep that channel clean and healthy. Remember, YOU are NOT giving anything to anyone as NONE of this is yours, to begin with! You are here to channel the energy of love from the Universe while connecting to that unlimited source yourself.

Chapter 4: SM Games We Like To Play

"He who has a 'why' for which to live can bear with almost any 'how'."

-Friedrich Nietzsche

~ Goddess Diana~

The story revolves around an old client that I refer to as Goddess Diana who became a walking well of pain and misery. Pain and misery were ready to spill over the sorrow of her own life, her previous lives, and the entire generations that came with her family. You got the point- she was the personification of misery itself, with her easy to water eyes, and her constantly broken heart. She grew up with a mother who was an emotionally strong and aggressive woman – the backbone of the family. Goddess Diana, was not fortunate enough to be her mom's favorite. It was her elder sister who enjoyed that position.

As a child, Goddess Diana quickly learned to bury her own beliefs and ideas, keeping them tightly packed inside her. She picked up and practiced every approach that would keep her far from conflicts and confrontations, even if it meant sacrificing her own ideas and beliefs. During this process, she ended up losing her own self, ultimately feeling empty inside. That void she filled with misery.

Once an adult, Goddess Diana entered into a joyless early marriage only to escape the tyranny of her mother. Yet again, she failed to explore what her heart ailed for. She spent a long span of fifteen years in the marriage just to realize that she is actually NOT attracted to men at all!

While her husband spent time at work she grew extremely close to her colleague and friend Goddess Baubo. The two goddesses together finally broke the expectations of society and formed a powerful union. Despite, such a brave step, Goddess Diana still could not find happiness as her voice was still shut. She was a helpless victim. Trying to please others, not stirring the waters, neglecting her own feelings- these became the tools that helped her survive in her miserable world.

My client came to me as her "last hope" and enrolled in my class to find her life's purpose. Once she understood that her pain of suppressing her sexual identity and her voice was the biggest gift which could be utilized to empower other individuals like her own self, she found her ultimate purpose. She is now helping like-minded individuals to stand in their power and embrace their sexuality and individuality. This has empowered her own self which has given rise to her own self-worth to a great extent. She is now in a much happier relationship where she expresses her needs and has the ability to stand for what she believes is right. She is even considering starting her own business helping LGBQT individuals to find their voice and power.

This story shows us one of the roles that we, humans, like to play. The role of victim, when we give complete control to other people or circumstances over our own lives and our own happiness. However, the victim role never comes alone. In this chapter, I will show you the sadomasochistic games we love to play and how they keep us away from experiencing our sexuality, creativity, pleasure, joy and life purpose.

According to Niel Burton (2014), "Sadomasochism refers to the giving or receiving of pleasure often sexual from the infliction or reception of pain or humiliation. It can enhance sexual pleasure or in some cases, it can serve as a substitute or sine qua non- as an essential condition. The infliction of pain is used to incite a sexual response, while the simulation of violence can form and express attachment. It connects the two sensations of pain and pleasure".

This chapter will focus on the psychological sadomasochistic games that we like to play. While some level of pain and torture might bring excitement to our lives, often we allow these tendencies to drown us psychologically and disconnect us from our authentic selves, separating us from our life purpose. Why do we like participating in behaviors that might hurt us? One answer is what I call "la Llorona effect".

La Llorona Effect

While we should listen to our pain to find our life purpose as we will discuss in chapter 5, we should be careful not to drown in the negative downward spiral. The negative pull in our society is actually a force that provides us with the energy to feed on the misery. Research backs this point of view. Negative stimuli trigger more neural activity in the brain. The amygdala, the brain region that regulates emotion and motivation makes use of two-thirds of its neurons to detect bad news.

This can be related to what I call "La Llorona effect". La Llorona is a Mexican folk heroine. According to the legend, she drowned her kids to get the attention of the man she loved. After realizing her bad deed, she started stealing kids from other families. Till this day she is doomed to continue walking, crying and stealing everyone's kids.

This legend is the perfect metaphor to describe what is happening in our world on the energetic level. While we gossip, get victimized or raise resentment towards others, we are stealing our chance of being happy. The feelings of hatred that rise in our hearts breed in the negativity, and feed on the pain and misery of others. All of this contributes to depriving us of attaining our higher purpose. We relate to La Llorona while iterating the same story again and again, when we house the feelings of hatred or resentment for others. While pain is a part of human's life, self-inducing or attaching to the pain is an unhealthy act. As a famous psychotherapist and Holocaust survivor Viktor E. Frankl perfectly stated, *"To suffer unnecessarily is masochistic rather than heroic."*

We should be careful of being stuck in a suffering mode and mistaking it with nobility, just as Frankl wrote: *"In some way, suffering ceases to be suffering at the moment it finds a meaning, such as the meaning of a sacrifice. But be careful of getting stuck in a suffering mode and mistaking it for nobility."*

Besides, the need to perpetuate our own suffering, human beings are also linked with the behaviors of deriving pleasure from giving pain to others. This ultimately causes self-destruction and keeps them deprived of attaining ultimate pleasure. Individuals get involved in masochistic behaviors which results in ruining them. These behaviors bring huge damage to our self-worth and our relationships with others. They disconnect us from our true calling and our life's purpose. Let's discuss the psychological behaviors of sadism and masochism that we are often engaged in.

The Sadistic Way Of Living

According to Michael Schreiner (2018), the sadistic way of living refers to delighting in cruelty. It revolves around the concept of taking pleasure from inflicting pain or suffering and humiliating others. It is not merely confined to the sexual sphere but encompasses a general life orientation. It is a way of seeing the world and relating to the living beings that reside in this world. Sadism manifests in personal and professional relationships, as well as interests, hobbies, beliefs and values.

Let's see how sadistic and masochistic tendencies interact and create co-dependent relationships.

Karpman Drama Triangle

The Kaprman Drama Triangle (1968) can help shed more light on the concept and the relationships that most adults are unconsciously engaged in their lives. These relationships are sadomasochistic by nature that ruin our lives and keep us away from feeling joy and purpose; yet most of us are not even aware of them. The triangle involves three components (or roles that most of us play). These are: victim, persecutor and the rescuer. Most adults can find themselves using one or more roles in their lives and have a predominant role in their relationships with others…and thus continuingly inflict pain on others and themselves.

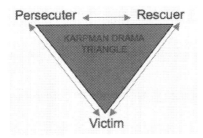

Figure 1. Karpman Drama Triangle

The persecutors: These are strong individuals who exert their power on the weaker, vulnerable ones. They are the ones who possess an ugly image of the world in their brain and find a way out of their frustration by exerting their power and influence on the weaker members of the society.

Who is the weaker one?

The victims: These the vulnerable ones who are made to believe that they have no voice and cannot stand up to the persecutors. They are usually misled and they easily drown in a world of misery and a feeling of helplessness all their lives (like Lisa in our story above). Their happiness and their lives depend on the outside circumstances and people.

The rescuers: These individuals will observe all the actions of the predator as well as the victim, and will invest their energy in bringing about a positive change and resolving the misbalance of power. The rescuer always remains in the good books of the victim for bringing a relief to the victim's life, who was unable to take an action for their own self. They often sacrifice their own happiness to make everyone else happy and believe that it is their role to save the situation.

This leads forward to a cycle where all three elements of the Kaprman Drama Triangle feel validated. This is a psychological "game" where the victim, predator and rescuer, each feel important. The victim cherishes the fact of receiving sympathy, while the rescuer feels good in helping out the victim. However, once the rescuer starts housing the thoughts that they are always on the giving end of the bargain, the feelings of help start turning into anger and frustration. This further paves the way forward where they stand on the position of the persecutor, inflicting pain on someone else, and eventually forcing the victim to swing into the role of the rescuer for someone else. This phase also throws the persecutor into a sea of guilt, where they drown in the state of misery and take up the position of the victim. The cycle continues and ultimately, each person falls back into their own favorite position.

After analyzing the dynamics of the Kaprman Drama Triangle, we can deduce that we are a part of the triangle without even being aware of it. For this purpose, it is important for us to get conscious of our participation in this game and ask ourselves the following questions:

❖ What kind of role do you prefer to play in various relationships – victim, predator, or a rescuer?

❖ How does being a predator, victim, or rescuer affect your daily life?

❖ Does it justify any kind of psychological necessities?

❖ Does it bring any kind of hindrance in your life?

❖ What is the nature of obstacles that you see (as a predator, victim, or a rescuer) in your life?

The purpose of understanding this triangle is not just to know your role, but it is to provide you with a solution. You need to come out of the triangle. Fall out of this cycle for which keeping a note or using any other mnemonic device might be helpful for you. I had a triangle drawn on my wrist for several months to keep reminding me to break free from the destructive cycle. Notice when you find yourself in a predator, victim or even a rescuer role, stop. This is important when you don't want to be sucked up solving negativities of your life, which would keep you at bay from achieving your life's purpose – the pleasure.

The Masochistic Way Of Living

Masochists derive pleasure from inflicting pain onto themselves, in our life we often use three self-destructive habits that keep us in misery and rob us of happiness. These are:

❖ Comparison

❖ Doubt

❖ Fear

Comparison

In today's era, when everyone is more aware of each other's life, the comparison has become an evil monster to welcome distress.

Jealousy is prevalent due to social media, where people aim at sharing better things happening in their lives which brings resentment, frustration and depression to their audience. Human beings enter into a vicious cycle of comparing themselves with others, whether consciously or unconsciously.

When we compare ourselves to others we go through several steps. *The first step* of the vicious cycle revolves around looking for the absence of something in our lives. This is not really based on the actual presence or absence of something but rather shows our perception. This perception of the "lack" makes the person feel frustrated and deprived of something important.

The second step leads us into the feeling of envy. We see others who possess what we perceive as missing in our lives and we experience a negative emotion towards that person.

The third stage is an unconscious passive-aggressive reaction, which leads a person into thinking that others are not worthy of the success that they are achieving. It makes the person think that it is fine to belittle others.

These behaviors and thoughts create a lot of challenges in our own lives. Comparisons create blocks and hindrances in our ability to progress and try to do new things. It also develops distrust in the environment, others, and ultimately the world.

However, it is important to remember that we ONLY envy those people that have something we can also have.

For example, if you don't care about playing tennis, you would not likely be jealous of the famous player Anna Kournikova, but if you like to dance, you might be jealous of someone who is a great dancer. So instead of either allowing yourself to fill your heart with envy, or suppressing the feeling, observe it and welcome it. Then remind yourself that the very fact that you experience envy means you can have the same as them too!!

Homework:

- Never ever repress envy, instead embrace it. Write the names of those people who you are envious of or who you compare yourself with. What gifts do they hold for you?

- Write down the description of emotions that you experience in that comparison state.

- Scroll through Facebook. See who do you compare yourself with and why?

- What are some hidden gifts of yours do these people reflect?

- When you feel envy, repeat the following mantra:

"How great! I also want _____ (fill in the blank with what you are supposedly missing), I also can _____ (fill in the blank) this way. I admire this success, and I bless this success. I am happy and I am grateful that I live in this world where such success is possible. I am grateful that this success is shown to me as an example, which means this success is a part of my world too!"

Then bless the person you are envious of with the Hawaiian Ho'oponopono prayer: *"I love you and I am sorry. Please forgive me. Thank you."*

Doubt

While doubt can be a good tool to assess weaknesses and strive for more greatness, most people get absorbed by the negativity and sink into a downward spiral. This behavior leads a person into thinking that they are not worthy of praise or appreciation.

Often we experience doubt after we have been criticized by others…. The people who criticize you take away your energy, the energy which can be utilized to attain bigger objectives. The closer these people are to you the deeper the effect they would produce on your life. However, we need to remember that there are two categories of critics. I call them *fans* and *players*. Just like in a soccer match!

The *fans* are those who criticize the players all the time. They usually have never even stepped their foot on the soccer field but they always know how the players should be playing, right? The critics who have never been in your shoes are just like those fans. Do you really want to listen to what they have to say?

The other thing is with those who are actual players. These people might have done what you are trying to accomplish and succeeded in areas where you are trying to succeed. Their criticism might be useful as they might have some good advice for you. However, most critics in our lives are not of this type.

So the first step to take when someone criticizes you is to stop and see- who is giving you their opinion? A player or a fan? You can most confidently ignore any criticism from the fans- this will be the majority of them in your life. But if the player gives you criticism- stop and think- maybe they are right? Maybe they are guiding you towards improvement, or maybe they can teach you how to improve that area of your life?

In summary, you can easily transcend any criticism and avoid awakening your doubts by doing the following:

❖ Anchor yourself by always analyzing and thinking rationally. Who is criticizing you? A player? A fan?

❖ Remember to ignore fan's criticism. It can simply be ignored without causing a problem and in a peaceful manner. Players, on the contrary, can be asked for advice or invited to collaborate.

Fear

Fear is one of the strongest emotions which can inhibit our growth and stop us from achieving success. This makes it important for us to be friends with this feeling so that we can accelerate our growth process. In our society, we learn to avoid feeling fear, yet the bravest men of all experience fear all the time. Nelson Mandela put it beautifully, *"I learned that courage was not the absence of fear, but the triumph over it. The brave man is not he who does not feel afraid, but he who conquers that fear."* Fear is here to protect us, but most importantly, it shows us the direction of our progress and points out to our life purpose.

What if I told you that fear is the red marker on the treasure map of your life that shows you the precise location where you biggest riches are buried?

Therefore, when you feel scared, consider it a great sign! It means you are heading towards your expansion because growth and fear go hand in hand. You don't grow somewhere you are comfortable. Therefore, rather than running away from fear, you need to befriend it. You can use the following creative process I use with my clients:

❖ First of all, paint your fear. Select a marker or a paint and let your hand draw it. Don't let your head control it, rather let it go on its own. What you paint should be an outcome of what your heart is feeling. Once you are done, see the portrait that you have created. It is your fear. You now have a physical picture of it in front of you which helps you to identify your emotions. Take a look at this picture. Then, name it. Yep, like "Mike" or "Poverty" or "Old Lady". Assigning a name to your fear is actually the trick which helps you give it an identity. Once it has an identity, you get a clear picture of what you are facing. You can use your Hawaiian prayer again while referring to this fear: *"Forgive me. I am sorry. I love you. I am grateful."*

Repeat this several times. It should feel a lot better now.

❖ Secondly, you should draw *gratitude*. Take red, yellow and blue colors and draw gratitude for your fear on the paper. You should follow your intuition and let it be painted in whatever direction your hand wants to move. After you are done you have to write down what this gratitude means to you.

❖ Third, you need to sign a contract with your fear. Yes, you read that correctly. You are going to sign a beautiful contract with your fear. You are going to write:

Dear Fear, _____. I am extremely grateful to you for

1. _____

2. _____

3. _____

4. _____

5. _____

(In these blanks, you need to write the reasons of being grateful to your fear.)

*I am planning to feel good about you by*_____
_____ (In this blank you write about the strategy that you are going to opt in order to befriend your fear).

Note: This paragraph is supposed to make you feel excited and scared at the same time. It should make you go "WOO-HOO" but at the same time, something inside your stomach should churn.

After that write the following:

I promise that I will do _____ (fill in the blank after picturing yourself in a certain desired state).

Note: Is there fun in the words that you have just written? It is supposed to excite you like a little child. This is how you trick your mind.

Then you finish it off:

I understand, that moving in this direction means moving
out of my comfort zone and that you are going to warn
and guide me at every step towards my dream. Now I

know that what is not scary for me is not interesting for me and probably not apart of my higher purpose.

Now put the date and sign it!

This activity will make you feel a lot better and will help you become friends with your fear.

To summarize, in this chapter we focused on behaviors that prevent us from truly enjoying ourselves, our lives and from finding our purpose. These behaviors while not sexual in nature are similar to the sadomasochistic tendencies that many people use in bed to make their sexual life more arousing. Just like in the sexual context, there is a thin line between excitement and danger that these behaviors possess. You must be aware of self-destructive behaviors and learn how to transcend them. In the following chapter, we will talk about how to channel your pain to access your life purpose and bring joy back into your life.

Chapter 5: From Pain to Pleasure

"Sadness gives depth. Happiness gives height. Sadness gives roots. Happiness gives branches. Happiness is like a tree going into the sky, and sadness is like the roots going down into the womb of the earth. Both are needed, and the higher a tree goes, the deeper it goes, simultaneously. The bigger the tree, the bigger will be its roots. In fact, it is always in proportion. That's its balance."

-Osho

~ Goddess Apsaras ~

Goddess Apsaras was a young lady in her early 20s. Tall and slender she walked elegantly as her long arms were moving gracefully as if she was flying. Her dark skin glowing, her short hair emphasizing the length of her neck making her look like a gorgeous dark swan.... Yet instead of freedom, she exuded pain and suffering. The second I asked her to share her story she started crying. She shared that all her life she felt very badly about herself. Her self-esteem was low and her partners used her and abused her. In fact, the last partner broke her nose so she had a small bump on her otherwise perfectly aligned face. While this bump gave her appearance some charm, it was a constant reminder of the suffering she had with her relationships and with herself. After our first session, she called me late at night telling me that while she went on her usual run, she suddenly had an explosion of emotions- all together.

She didn't remember when she had cried so hard and so loud in all her life (even when she was abused) she was kept quiet, afraid to make anyone mad. In all of this mixture of emotions she suddenly realized that she had abandoned the one thing that mattered most to her—dancing. As she was courageous enough to dive into her pain, she found the answers she could not find for years. And as she became OK expressing her feelings, her body followed up by reminding her that she needs to dance.

She was a dancer since she was a child and even performed and competed professionally for years. Then, after her first breakup, she abandoned dancing and buried it so deeply in her heart that she could not understand the true reason for her depression. She was NOT dancing. That was her cure- to start moving. So easy, yet so hard to understand under layers of suppressed emotions.

Pain And Pleasure

The relationship between pain and pleasure exists – just like there would be no plausible explanation of light without darkness, and no gratification of sound and melody without dissonance and cacophony. Common sense implores us to seek pleasure and avoid pain at all costs, but we not always get what we want, do we?

There is a polarity and dichotomy that lives in each of us and stirs our curiosity. It is not unusual for us to give in to situations that we fear, circumstances in which we anticipate the worst.

Replacing our tendency of avoidance with a capacity to embrace can relieve our suffering and allow us to release an untapped capacity for pleasure.

What happens every time we engage in sexual intercourse? We are jolted by ecstasy which releases insurmountable pleasure and stimulates an equal release of intense pain. The pelvic cavity, one of the most astounding wonders in the human body, mediates between the ability to walk erect, properly and procreate. It is that internal vacuum where sensation is the leader and I have often pondered what begets what; if it is actually the intensity of the pain that arouses the pleasure or the other way round. Scientists have discovered pain in the same brain circuits which releases pleasure. In fact, love, sex, pain, and violence all serve as catalysts to release similar chemicals and hormones in the human body.

According to S. Leknes and I. Tracey (2008) there are extensive similarities in the anatomical substrates of painful and pleasant sensations. Endorphins (the pleasure-giving hormones) released during painful experiences are often perceived as pleasured. There are logical and scientific data to support why people engage in mild violence and sadistic foreplay before sex. Stress and pain also stimulate serotonin and melatonin, which are responsible for the transformation of our painful emotions into pleasurable ones. Similarly, the release of epinephrine and norepinephrine during pain can also bring about a pleasurable *'dash'*. Normal human biological responses actually support the intricate and mysterious fibre between pain and pleasure, which is evident in our facial expressions during the release of orgasm.

The question begging to be asked is, *"Why are some forms of pain enjoyable, while others just plain agonizing?"*

One theory that that aims to explain is *"benign masochism"* (Rozin, et. al., 2003) – seeking out pain while being conscious that it will not cause severe mental or physical damage. It is something that we humans, who have intuition and cognitive abilities are capable of. This theory also explains why we seek out and enjoy other unpleasant episodes, such as fear-inducing roller coasters, poignant movies, consumption of alcohol, etc... These are types of hedonic reversal, the conversion of a (usually) innate negative experience into a positive experience and can be referred to as *"glad to be sad"*. *"If an animal took a rollercoaster ride, it would be scared and would never go again,"* says Paul Rozin. However, we humans, like tortuting ourselves as long as we know we are safe. Women, according to the researchers, are even more inclinded to this type of benign masochism, especially to sadness in movies, songs, etc...

Another theory connects sex and pain. Some of us use sex for pure pleasure, while others use it as an outlet to relieve themselves of the afflictions they are going through. However, it is important to note that the sex and pain are not only confined to the domain of BDSM. One study found that cancer survivors, who had nerves in their spinal cord cut to relieve abdominal pain, lost the ability to have orgasms - implying that if their pain returned, so would the orgasms! Another observation asserts that facial expressions during orgasms are often indistinguishable from those in pain. So, for human beings, we can say that pain and pleasure are always woven together.

According to Wendy Strgar (2011), given our physiology and anatomical makeup, it does not come as a surprise that the practice of combining painful techniques with sexuality is archaic. Roman poets, aristocrats, and even the now-famous Kama Sutra all advocate sexual practices, which in the present aeon have come to be known as BDSM. This acronym reflects the ancient sex rituals and practices of dominance and submission that have qualified as normal sex throughout history. Taking one study into account, the percentage of people who are engaged in this technique range from 10-25%. Interestingly, this figure is matched by an equally significant percentage of people who avert from being sexually active due to the fear of pain associated with sex.

Looking at how our sexual experience is mirrored in the emotions of relationship offers an eye-opening outlook. This is what Wendy proposes:

Loving someone emotionally creates the same pain/pleasure experience that resides in the body while making physical love to them. The moments of deep connection and intimacy, vulnerability, and nakedness are matched by their opposite experience: the ability to feel deeply hurt and emotionally shattered by what was said, or have been done by our partner. The act of endearing in whatever form requires a willingness to experience both pleasure and pain in doses. This is the foundation of sustaining, loving relationships that are easy to miss out on, or at least misunderstood. It is also often the experience which we walk away from depriving our heart of what it yearns the most.

The Cost Of The Avoidance Of Pain

When it comes to dark or negative emotions, we are all experienced sufferers: - grief, fear, pain, and loss is our birth-right just as much as joy, elation and love. There is no life without loss, no pleasure without pain, and no success without determination. Yet as logical as it sounds, our cultural conditioning and moral upbringing do not seem to reflect this world wisdom. Negative does not always mean bad – but as a culture, we have shrouded these emotions in the dark, the unseen realm. But if we keep suppressing our emotions, they truly turn into darkness – a very different form of darkness.

In the United States, it is commonly believed that giving negative emotions too much space is a sign of emotional fragility. Nevertheless, there have been numerous treatises and scientific findings that showcase that we need the right mix of emotions in our life. We need to react in a specific way to events and behaviors of others. Let us say, you have a lifelong friend, whom you have enjoyed quality time with and confided all your secrets to -- betrays you for a different person. How would you react? Of course, you would express dissent, frustration, and dismay. This is how the brain is programmed to function. Now, had you pretended that it did not bother you- this very act of pretending would create an imbalance in the functioning of your brain and the chemicals it produces. It would also create a block in your energetic system as we learned in chapter 2.

In the US, when things seem to fall apart for people, we give into feelings of embarrassment and guilt. Americans love to say *"I do not want to put this on you".* Now, this is something I would never hear in my native Russia. How many times do you hear your friend telling you about their own negative experience (if they are ever going to share it with you) constantly followed by '*sorry*'. What are they sorry about? Feeling bad because they broke up with a loved one or lost a parent? Why do we have the need to apologize? Because we have been culturally conditioned that **we would rather render ourselves dead and lifeless to our emotions than actually go through them.**

We would rather get addicted to mood enhancing drugs (that by the way do not really get rid of sadness they just kill all emotions, positive emotions including, turning us into walking, talking zombies), or recreational drugs, or food, or anything else outside of ourselves.

Why are we schooled to turn away from these emotions instead of accepting them as normal, behavioral responses? Many research studies show that Americans want to avoid negative states of beings more than other cultures do. The cultural message that "*You should feel good and avoid feeling bad.*" is one of the most vitriolic pieces of advice in modern psychology. Americans are not particularly fond of openly expressed anger, sadness, guilt, and similar other negative emotions. While in other countries, for example, if you are asked the question, "*How are you?*" it is perceived as an invitation to open up and share your sadness, joy, anger, and happiness, Americans have an aversion from such emotional expressions, which makes adapting to this culture very difficult for many foreigners. So it is time to start befriending that beast!

Despite the numerous attempts to find solutions to completely eliminate pain from our lives: through alcohol, drugs, anti-depressants, counseling and even spiritual practice, the pain is not going to go away. You can call it a necessary evil of life. Even more, it is the surest way to your life purpose. Yes, you heard me correctly.

Pain is actually the best road to finding your life purpose. We are often so quick to form judgment of a certain situation and run away from the pain that even without knowing it, we cut the flow of good things in our lives.

But remember, judging events as positive or negative is like cheapening an expensive fragrance.

Much like musical notes make up a song and various shades of colors turn into a painting, fragrance notes are necessary to make a perfume. Overall, there are three note scales that when blended together create the perfume's fragrant accord. The top notes are recognized immediately upon application of the perfume, the heart notes, make an appearance once the top notes evaporate. The middle notes are considered the heart of the fragrance. They last longer than the top notes and have a strong influence on the base notes to come. The base notes are the final fragrance notes that appear once the top notes are completely evaporated. Without the combination of the three levels of notes, a fragrance just wouldn't be aromatically as appealing and would lose their "expensive" "sophisticated" quality. But together, they create beautiful scents.

So is the case with life, some events that seem scary or painful might turn out to be rewarding in the future. By judging the event as negative and escaping from it, we neglect the main treasures of life and cut ourselves off from the universal guiding energy. We need to allow circumstances to unravel themselves and wait for them to reveal their deeper meaning.

From Pain To Pleasure And Life Purpose

The usual approach in psychology to finding your life purpose is: - *"Your Values + Strengths + Passions + Service = Your Purpose".* But the key ingredient that is missing here is – *'pain'* and thus this new spiritual/ sexual/ existential concept is needed to find what our biggest trigger points are, that give meaning to our life. As Rumi stated, *"The cure for pain is in the pain itself."*

Our emotions are not just ours, they are connectors and vessels to the universe and beyond. Through them, we can achieve the *'oneness'* that our souls crave. By becoming one with what surrounds us, we can understand the suffering of our ancestors and make sense of our history, traditions, and lineage.

In most non-Christian or indigenous cultures, darkness is always needed for the light to spread its aura. In old Slavic folklore, for example, *'Belobog'* is the white God, and embodies sunshine, passion, warmth, and life. His followers offer him prayers and rituals to seek guidance through dark forests and to bring about the healthy crop. Belobog is imagined as having a bright, bearded countenance, carrying a staff and heralded in white robes. He only appears during the daylight, helping his men achieve success and prosperity.

As the myth goes, he was said to battle his twin brother, *'Chernobog'*, the black God, twice a year to maintain order. Chernobog was associated with bleak and odious attributes, such as cold, famine, poverty and disease. During the creation of the world, many contend that the two titans came into conflict and their polarizing actions created the cycles of the universe (night & day, summer & winter and the motion of the stars). Chernobog rules over the darker half of the year, while Belobog presides over the brighter half. The analogy here I hope is clear to you, they both are needed in their subtle ways, to keep the cycle of the Universe going.

Similarly, in Hinduism, Brahma, Vishnu and Shiva are considered to be the most powerful deities. Brahma is the creator, Vishnu is the preserver and Shiva is the destroyer. Shiva is the harbinger of destruction and an important part of the Trinity as, without destruction, there can be no recreation. In pictures and scriptures, Shiva is represented as Lord of the Dance who controls the movements of the Universe. He is also associated with fertility, which again is linked to sex, destruction, pain, and life.

These ideas are innate in all of us humans and are all interrelated. Research shows that when we are close to experiencing death, we feel alive and that pain is closely connected with arousal. Hence the phrase, *"Death is the ultimate orgasm of life."* An experiment called, *"The Suspension Bridge Experiment"* was conducted by Donald Dutton and Arthur Aron in 1974, in order to demonstrate a process where people apparently misjudged the cause of a higher level of arousal. The outcomes showed that men who were approached by alluring females on a less secure bridge were found to experience a higher level of arousal. Thus, danger and proximity to death increased the attraction factor of women. In his best selling book titled *The Upside of your Dark Side* (2015) Dr. Todd Kashdan argues that being your whole self not just your *"good self"* puts you on the path to success and fulfillment and clears the road towards your life purpose.

So pain is just as integral in our life like every other emotion and has a great potential to help us find the true meaning of life. One such person who found the true purpose in his sufferings was Holocaust survivor Viktor Frankl. Frankl and his family, in 1942, were deported to the Nazi Theresienstadt Ghetto. His mother, brother and wife died at the concentration camp. The only other survivor he had with him was his sister. In the midst of his suffering and horrific experiences of going through a tremendous amount of pain, loss of freedom and mental annihilation, Frankl managed to connect with his core and found the meaning of life and the purpose of his soul. Here is what he wrote about this astounding revelation:

"...In some way, suffering ceases to be suffering at the moment it finds a meaning, such as the meaning of a sacrifice."

So it is incredibly important to be able to dive into your pain and unpleasant periods in your life in order to find your honest self and your meaning. Just like in yoga, when we stretch, the first reaction of our body is to squeeze and resist the pain, but the yogis teach you to breathe and relax into the pain as when we do this, a passage opens up, a passage that we have not even thought possible. Endless possibilities to reach a higher existence open their doors to us, the question is, are you willing to go through pain and embrace the flaws in you? Are you ready to accept the darker side of you to finally understand and embrace the purpose of your life?

Chapter 6: Find the G Spot of Your Soul

Wife: 'Honey, look at this amazing cherry tree blossoming right in front of our kitchen window in the backyard!'

Husband: 'Yes, my love...it has been here for 13 years...you just did not notice.'"

-From my client Goddess Oya

~ Goddess Oya~

Goddess Oya came to me three years ago, horrified at her predicament. She was diagnosed with bipolar depression many years ago and as a result, was on several heavy duty drugs for over thirteen years. These drugs made her condition even worse. All they managed to accomplish was to make her feel numb to her environment for a limited amount of time. They killed both the negative and the positive emotions, as her unresolved issues were buried deeper and deeper in her soul causing an enormous amount of pain and messing up her professional and personal life.

In the initial stages of her so-called 'recovery', she started missing her project deadlines. Weeks went by and she could not even complete the projects that began a month ago. She became so frustrated with the corporate job that she only went to the office in order to maintain formality. Although this was her dream job back in the day, she had become disoriented towards it in a relatively short span of time.

The medicines had shown their ultimate mastery over Goddess Oya's will when she decided to say farewell to her occupation. She had enough of the corporate culture and could not bear the thought of working endlessly in order to increase her productivity. She could not tolerate it anymore and decided to leave it once and for all. She had hoped that her decision would benefit her mental health, but instead, her condition became worse than ever before, as now she was stressing over money.

Goddess Oya had tried everything, therapies, hypnosis, and self-help books. Yet nothing sufficed and her descent into depravity increased at an exponential rate. Just when Goddess Oya thought that all doors were closed for her, she came to me and asked for my counsel.

Goddess Oya got enrolled in my course and after taking a series of my coaching sessions, she finally began to establish some manner of harmony in her life. She did this with one simple thing; aligning herself with her real purpose. It took her a while to shed all the expectations of others that she had carried in her psyche and connect with her unique purpose, which was none other than writing! She had been aware of her true calling for a long time, but she did not pursue it in light of the pressures of her family and society as a whole. As soon as she got a hold of her purpose, everything began falling in line for Goddess Oya.

Her depression and mental deterioration became a thing of the past and she began exploring her options. It almost seemed as if the universe was smiling down upon her, as new and better opportunities began to emerge in her life out of thin air. All of a sudden, Goddess Oya started getting clients from all walks of life. Her literary pursuits had developed a positive word of mouth and she started to gain recognition for her efforts. Goddess Oya's clientele began growing exponentially, up until the point that she started receiving media coverage. She became an instant hit and attended book signings, received awards and got invited onto radio and TV programs in lieu of her new rapid rise to fame. Goddess Oya finally had everything she ever wanted, all because she started to pursue her soul's purpose.

Even her doctor had second thoughts about her diagnosis thirteen years ago and told her that her condition was probably a misdiagnosis as Goddess Oya did not show any signs of mental disturbance or anxiety. Perhaps, my client's greatest achievement would be to gaze upon the cherry tree that was growing right across her window. She finally caught a glimpse of it, despite the tree being there for many years. This only happened because she learned her true purpose in life. So now, we will ponder over the different factors involved in her attaining spiritual and emotional bliss.

In this chapter, we will discuss this concept even further and try to decipher what is needed for a person to find their soul's G-Spot. This is the core essence of our spiritual anatomy. As a result, it must have an outlet. For that, we need to get closely acquainted with our emotional and psychological selves. It's not by chance that the only phrase on the temple of Apollo in Delphi, Greece (the place famous for the oracles who could see into the future) was *"Know Thyself"*.

What is the G-Spot of Your Soul?

Each and every individual on the face of the Earth has a soul, and that soul needs a purpose. It does not have to be magnanimous or astounding. It could be very simple, but we must fulfill it. **Our purpose in life is simply to become a channel of the divine energy (which is God, the universe, higher self- or whatever you call it). This energy runs through every being in the world. We are here to express this light in the way that is unique to us.** Yet we rarely do it and as a result we are out of flow, pushing, striving and suffering.

In order to understand this, we can take the example of a hammer and an alarm clock. The alarm clock serves its purpose by helping us to wake up and meet our obligations all the while a hammer is used to push in nails. If we switch both of their purposes, they will never be able to fulfill them.

This scenario applies in our lives perfectly as progressing through, while living another individual's purpose, will never feel like *"flowing"* and will not bring fulfillment. We are inherently born as diamonds, which are unique, rough and precious. Society, on the contrary, teaches us to become rhinestones that have a glittery or shiny exterior, yet they are fragile on the inside because of their plastic base.

During our childhood, everyone near and dear to us is concerned with what our purpose is supposed to be. They constantly ask two questions; what do you want to be and how do you want to achieve it? Yet, at the same time when they ask these questions, they also answer them for us. They provide a guideline on how our life should progress and what we should do in order to fit in the perfect spectrum of society.

As a result, we completely lose track of our own unique purpose and start a journey trying to live according to other people's expectations. We get detached from our calling because according to our parents or other "advisors" our passion would not guarantee profits or financial abundance. We lose track of the fact that we are souls who have come into this world to shine and show our impeccable brilliance. We lose sight of our ultimate goal and put all our efforts into securing financial stability. Even if we manage to achieve said stability, we will still be depressed and lack fulfillment.

The desires that society as a whole finds awkward or disorientating are vital factors that make us human. These urges are present in every human being, no matter how much they try to deny them. These desires not only shape us into what we are today, but they also propel our emotional and spiritual growth. It all depends upon the individual; whether they suppress their desires and run the risk of losing their identity or they choose to express their needs and eventually discover their spiritual G Spot.

In my experience, by the time we turn twenty we build so many layers between our authentic brilliance and so-called *"adult version of our purpose"* that it becomes next to impossible to peel those layers off on our own. You must remember that your core brilliance is not just your talents or skill set. It is also your soul's spark, the qualities that you might be ashamed of. This is what living in the G Spot is all about; you need to accept all of these qualities and only then you will be able to truly shine, to truly be that diamond.

If you are reading these words and have no idea what is your life purpose, don't worry! You are definitely not alone. Research suggests that finding our cause for existence (aka aligning with your true self) is the most tumultuous journey that a human being can encounter. Scholars believe that discovering purpose is an arduous and stress-inducing process, yet it proves to be fruitful in the longer run. According to Frankl (1963), the search process for finding purpose is the cause for tension, frustration and distress. He termed this form of existential distress as *"noogenic neurosis."* Yes, it is neurosis indeed when we live everyone's dreams and speak everyone's voices instead of our own!

Unfortunately, many of us are under the false impression that the outside material and physical world will solve our inner turmoil, which only leads to the problem exacerbating and turning into a full-fledged disease. The vicious cycle of finding a job, earning money and repeating the same old redundant process has taken a huge toll on our lives. We have gotten used to this routine so much that we do not have the time or urge to pursue anything other than this monotonous cycle. Family, peers, colleagues and network circles play a huge role in submerging our identity into this useless repetitive structure.

Women, in particular, suffer the most from not attaining or connecting with their true purpose in life. This is because many women as we talked about before are programmed to live FOR someone else: for their kids, their husbands, their jobs. There is just no time for such "frivolities" as looking for a life purpose in a woman's life. However, women who do not live according to their own unique purpose literally die on the inside. All the while, when a woman connects to her purpose she starts living in the flow and her energy keeps replenishing on its own so she is able to retain her youthfulness, strength and beauty.

When a person truly lives *in the G Spot,* they are happy, shiny, joyful and kind. They are also kind of wild and maybe not as "perfect" as the society wants them to be. They have rough edges, they don't conform and they definitely are able to say "NO" to events, circumstances and people who don't support their path. This is because, as the saying goes, a genius domesticated is a genius lost. You should never dim your light and should never try to tame your brilliance. Once you accept your purpose, you will start shedding unnecessary layers of discomfort and rise to anew like a phoenix. The journey might not be comfortable or convenient, as it will bring lots of tests for you in this chaotic world and its many imperfections. This is because this world is the best spiritual teacher you can have and you should use it to clean your system and remove any clutters from your channel of energy.

Now let us look at the physical definition of the G Spot. The G Spot is the inner vaginal wall of a woman that is both, erogenous and provides a capable point for achieving ejaculation or pleasure. Many women have difficulty finding this spot, and thus, pleasure comes as a result of pain, and efforts coming together in a beautiful way.

Spiritually, pleasure is a portal for a transcendental experience that is really just pure freedom from worries and all restrictions. It is a means of having spiritual truth within our body. When we view an orgasm in the light of esotericism, it is the ultimate release for all stagnant old beliefs. It connects us with the flow of the universe and becomes the true diamond spot of our life.

As discussed previously, the society tries to dim our diamond into a simple rhinestone. The rhinestone is one dimensional due to its exterior beauty and interior hollowness or lack of structure. In the modern day, people strive to become one-dimensional rhinestone as they are under the false pretence that the external image is all that matters. But the true purpose is like a true diamond, it's multi-dimensional. So let's use this multi-dimensionality to find your soul's G Spot.

Let's find the G-Spot of Your Soul!

For your convenience, I created a formula for finding your purpose that I visually depicted in a shape of a diamond (see Figure 2). This formula revolves around two major principles. The first principle is truly realizing your full potential which includes reviewing your particular talents, interests and most of all strengths. The second core principle involves finding your potential and using that attribute to serve others and make their lives better. This is a VERY important role, if you remember, your life purpose is really not yours- you are just a channel of the divine energy that is manifested through you to serve others.

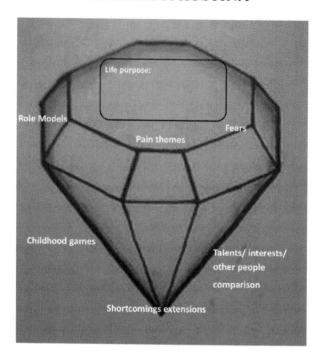

Figure 2: The Diamond Formula for Finding Your Soul's G-spot

Since your soul is as multi-dimensional and precious as a diamond, just like a diamond it has a lower and upper area. The lower part is your talents, while the upper area is dedicated to the service you give to others. The lower part of this diamond consists of three factors that include the games we played in our childhood, the shortcomings we felt throughout our lives and the talents/interests that we hold dear to us.

Similarly, the upper part also consists of three variables which help the person fulfill their service to others. The three variables are the role models we admire, the pain we experience in our journey, and the fears and insecurities we possess. As mentioned previously, pain, fears and shortcomings are vital to attaining our purpose because they shape our persona for the better and they show us what really matters in our lives.

So, are you ready to complete the diamond formula to find your true G-Spot? I will guide you through each step of this process.

Lower Part Of The Diamond

Step 1: Childhood Games

Childhood games are imperative for knowing your true purpose. As I mentioned above, as kids we are much more connected to our dreams and true soul's desires than when we become adults and absorb other people's views and opinions of us. As a child, you understood your innate purpose in a more realistic sense. You must ask yourself three questions:

a. What games did you like to play as a child? _____

_____

_____

_____

_____

b. What did you like to play even if your parents didn't allow you to? _____

_____

_____

_____

_____

c. What was the reason for playing those games? _____

_____

_____

_____

_____

When you have an answer to these questions you will be one step closer to finding your purpose. In my case, I liked to play more boys games as a child, such as being a musketeer because I had a huge need to find justice, help others and protect the less fortunate.

Step #2: Talents:

In this section, we will list all the talents that you are aware of about yourself. You can identify this by recalling in your mind what action or daily occupation you like doing the most, and feel like you are good at. These talents could be 25 all the way to 30. Reread the list and circle the first five that jump from the page louder than others and feel very good to your heart.

Your top 5 talents:

1. _____

2. _____

3. _____

4. _____

5. _____

Step 3: Shortcomings:

Next, we will discuss our so-called shortcomings and how they propel us to our unique purpose. These are actually reflections of your talents also, they are just not as obvious to identify as the ones above. In this part, you need to identify and confess your most annoying shortcomings and then adopt the "minus to plus technique". What do I mean by that? The minus to plus technique involves identifying the shortcoming and realizing that it is in actuality a blessing in disguise. I will give you my example so that you can grasp this concept more easily. I always thought of myself as a huge procrastinator. Despite being an active person I would find many ways to delay my projects or tasks. Sometimes I would take the whole day and just watch movies and read books, and at times I literally could not get out of bed (and had to call in sick to work). Being a responsible person by nature I obviously could not stand that feature of mine and prayed to be able to get rid of it. Often I forced myself to be active in those times but I only found myself to be completely exhausted and unproductive at the end.

As I progressed in my life, I found out that my procrastination was an extension of one of my most important strengths. It was the direct result of my innate creativity. Any creative person can understand me when I say that when I had my muse, I would work and create non-stop; days, nights, forgetting to sleep and food. My procrastination actually kept me sane and alive as no one can last without sleep and food forever! I needed time doing absolutely nothing in order to relax and recharge my mind and replenish my creative talents.

So make a list of your shortcomings and write down their beautiful extensions, your biggest gifts right next to them:

Shortcoming ---------------→ Gift

_____   _____

_____   _____

_____   _____

_____   _____

_____   _____

Upper Part Of The Diamond

Step 4: Influences:

We will now embark upon the higher part of the diamond diagram which is concerned with your service to others. First, we will find your role models. List five to seven role models below. Figure out what you like about them and what role do they play in the lives of other people. For instance, I have always admired Wayne Dyer. Not just because he was a renowned spiritual figure and knew how to motivate other people. I admired Wayne Dyer because he gave his audience the tools to live their true potential and truly inspired others. This purpose appeals to me dearly as I share the same purpose in life although I accomplish this through my own personal attributes.

Now list your figures of inspiration and the reasons you are inspired by them:

Person   Their contribution

1. _____   _____

2. _____   _____

3. _____   _____

4. _____   _____

5._____   _____

Step 5: Pain:

This step is the most difficult one as it requires you to search and reflect upon your painful experiences. You need to identify why such experiences keep occurring in your life, the underlying deeper meaning behind these occurrences and how they reflect what really matters to you. You can use these tools to help others deal with similar situations. Remember, in the beginning of the book I shared how my failed relationships and lack of money reflected my deeper challenge- lack of self-love. Once I realized that these experiences were not for my punishment but for my awakening- they helped me become aware of my issues and finally learn how to love myself. Now I am helping others find love where there is darkness. And so are YOUR painful experiences given to you as your most precious tool for returning back to yourself as they show what your values, interests and aspirations are. Each of us has a theme (or themes) of repeated painful patterns.

List them and try to understand what deeper meaning they have. You can go back to chapter five to review what you have written there.

Painful pattern   Its deeper meaning

_____   _____

_____   _____

_____   _____

Step 6: Fears:

The last step deals with the fears that you possess and how they propel you towards your purpose in life. Like we discussed in previous chapters the fear elements assist you in discovering your real potential in life. They are treasure maps to your ultimate destiny and you need to find a balance between your fear of something and your drive to achieving it. I, on a personal level, always had a fear of guiding masses of people and making them realize their purpose in life. I experienced tremendous fear of my purpose yet I wanted to achieve it nonetheless.

You must also recognize your three core fears. Afterwards, discover which direction they are pointing. Do you have a fear of public speaking? Do you have a fear of writing? Are you scared to be on camera? Are you afraid of being abandoned in a relationship? As you see fears are different for each of us.

Fear   Direction it is pointing

_____

_____

_____

_____

Put it all together:

I am so excited we approached this part! We are ready to put it all together to find your life purpose. Look at the steps one through six. Fill out all the core elements of the diamond diagram below. Now you need to put a researcher hat on as you are going to start seeing common "themes" that exist among all of these seemingly unrelated items. Write down these themes on the diamond's "sweet spot". Sleep on them! Literally walk away and let them stay there. Come back and look at them with fresh eyes. What do you see? What is that sweet spot of the diamond? What is the G-spot of your soul?

Once you discover it, hold it dear to your heart. It is your most precious gift. Cherish it and follow it regardless of society's opinion of it. If at this moment you have no idea what to do with it, don't worry. Soon enough the Universe will start opening doors for you, pointing you to the right people, books, courses and will guide you to fulfilling your most important desire- your soul's desire, the G-spot of your soul.

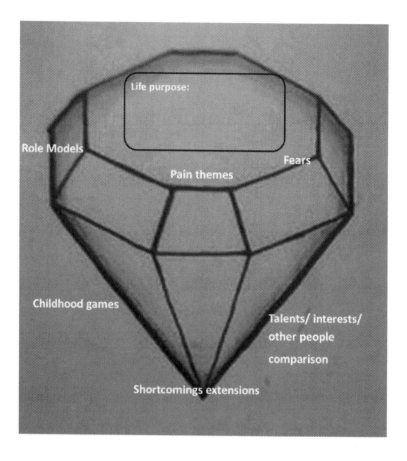

Chapter 7: The Pass to Your Multi-Orgasmic Soul

"Find what you love and let it kill you."

-Charles Bukowsky

~ Goddess Chokmah~

Goddess Chokmah was a Spanish lady who came to the states six years ago. During these years she did everything she could in order to survive in the new culture- she washed dishes, worked as a babysitter, worked as a clerk while pulling herself through school. She finally got her dream corporate job but something was missing. She realized that all these years of dreaming to have a big office downtown Chicago was actually not something her freedom-loving nature wanted. Cement, glass, and iron of the buildings became a cage for her free-spirited nature. And despite warnings and advice from her friends, she decided to take a leap of faith.... And she quit her marketing position to become a children's clothes designer!

She walked out of that office feeling empowered and proud of herself. She had just claimed to the universe her life mission and surely the Universe was going to start opening all the doors for her!

The excitement subsided very fast after on the first day of walking away from her soul-wrenching job she lost her wallet and found a parking ticket staring at her on her car... What? This was not according to plan. She was expecting a completely opposite picture. *"What is wrong with you, Universe?"*, - she muttered

Then just after a week the condo association where she lived hit her with a special assessments bill that would have wiped away a huge chunk of her savings. Goddess Chokmah came to me in tears and in complete disappointment with herself, the world, and the Universe. She could not understand, how after making such a brave statement she got so punished?

My client is not alone. Many people find themselves in this situation and I want to dedicate this chapter to the discussion of circumstances where our life purpose seemingly leads us into more trouble, so you are aware of what is going on and adjust accordingly without losing your course!

Why does your life journey slap you hard when you want to make a sincere effort in following your heart's desires?

One of my spiritual mentors, Megan Hamilton, introduced the concept of *ricochet* to me. Such difficult situations occur as a result of the *ricochet effect* of existence.

We human beings are programmed in a way that attracts us towards routines and familiarity. Although new events and situations spark our curiosity, we usually want the same routines to occur on a continuous basis. This is because our brain knows only one way to survive, and that is by forming habits and familiar practices. These habits even include negative, emotional and societal experiences, such as attracting abusive partners or doing nothing to alter our financial condition. This is because habits assist us in getting through each day of our existence. Habits save us from overthinking about routine tasks, such as brushing our teeth, making tea, driving and other basic actions. This is how the human brain operates, and there is little we can do to alter this situation.

Blame It On Ganglia

If you are looking for someone to blame in this scenario, blame the basal ganglia; the region of the brain which controls our habits, addictions and procedural learning. As soon as we create any new habit, the neural activity in this region also alters its course. The same case applies when we change a particular habit.

Even if we break our habits, basal ganglia form them again whenever we are exposed to a familiar routine or practice. This occurs because it took a significant amount of effort for our brain to learn these routines in the first place. This is the logical explanation as to how negativity attracts us and forms an impregnable chain around us. Nevertheless, there is a spiritual element to these circumstances as well.

As a result of our tenacity, we try to alter our life at any given moment. When we make a sincere effort and adopt reasonable change, life propels us towards the same old routines and patterns.

This is because the ricochet effect takes its toll on our existence and presents us with situations that resemble our past.

Remember that everything is energy and as Wayne Dyer stated energetically we attract not what we want, but *what we are.* Once we want to break an old habit and start caring for ourselves, life seems to resemble a rubber band... It is almost like this ricochet effect tests you to see whether you will go back to the familiar, easy "paved road" or be willing to dive full force into the realm of the unknown...

Talking about paved roads...

In Tarot, the card of new beginnings is represented by The Fool. Interestingly, to see how the "path" of these new beginnings is depicted here. If we further study this card, we see a man that is facing northwest (which represents the unknown), has his gaze upwards towards the spirit (angel, universe or the sky), and is about to fall off from a cliff.

Picture 6: The Fool

This is a symbolic representation of change itself because altering our destiny often resembles falling from a cliff as we are completely oblivious to what the future holds for our life. Even if the change is something beneficial for us, like marriage, we will still experience a plethora of negative emotions because we are dramatically altering our life's pattern while being unaware of the implications or consequences. Yet keeping your eyes on the target and trusting the process is the key to success.

Modern research claims that human beings prefer to anticipate all consequences of a particular action. They want to know how a particular act will impact their lives and the lives of those near and dear to them. This is the reason why we are frightened at our core as soon as we comprehend the notion of falling down from a high area. This is also the reason why an individual experiences karmic situations, such as a breakup, money problems, sickness and pain as soon as he or she embarks upon their spiritual purpose by altering their old habits. Since most of us are too quick and judge the situation as negative (remember, we talked about this in previous chapters), we often give up.

As a result, we get distracted from our main objectives of finding the right person, starting a business, and letting go of our past patterns. All of this distractions develop into a negative mindset that tells us that we are not worthy of anything and that things will never change for the better. Although going through these tumultuous situations is hard and can completely paralyze you mentally, you still need to move forward as there is no other way to transform your destiny.

The only way to get through the ricochet effect is to go through it!

All of these impairments will turn out to be opportunities as soon as you adopt a new way of living. I can guarantee this scenario because I too suffered from the devastations of the ricochet effect. I also reverted back to my old toxic life pattern time and time again, until I discovered the reason for my stumble. I was looking for faults outside of myself while the problem lied deep within me. I changed my beliefs and addressed the underlying issues, by expanding my vision of myself within me. Then I watched as the universe granted me my wishes and filled that space I created with abundance. You could do the same by simply staying true to yourself and not running away in fear when things don't seem to go your way.

Life is filled with obstacles, no matter which path an individual chooses. So it is a much more viable option to spend one's resources in attaining actual happiness. We can all become phoenixes and rise from the ashes of self-doubt in order to chase our calling. Remember, in pursuing your purpose you are not only clearing your own karma, but you also brighten up the paths of many other people around you and make their lives happier and filled with light.

So what should you do when you encounter yourself in the ricochet effect? Here are two strategies that should help you make the ride through this turbulent time easier.

Align Yourself with the Universal Laws

The first strategy involves aligning yourself with the Universal laws that rule our existence. One of these laws involves the individual, you, following your spiritual path. In the moments of self-doubt, I invite you to follow these mantras and repeat them each time you are faced with difficulty.

a. Every time when I doubt myself that I have the right to realize my talents I am acting against all Universal laws…

b. Remember what I feel now is what I am going to attract.

c. Every time when I don't act because I believe that someone else has already done this before me, I am depriving the world of my genius and from the sources of diversity, a new source of goodness, creativity and love. Remember, one of the beautiful features of the universe is diversity.

d. Every time I don't act according to my soul's calling because I am afraid that others will not support me on my journey I demonstrate my lack of trust in the universe. Remember the line from Paolo Coehlo's Alchemist: "When you want something, all the universe conspires in helping you to achieve it". I don't need the approval of those negative few people in my life.

e. Every time I hear phrases such as "you cannot do it", "you are too… (fill in the blank)"—and agree with them believing in my failure, I accept that the opinion of one or several people is more important than the universal laws regarding me and my purpose here. What God knows about me is more important than what others think about me.

f. I, (put your name here) am responsible for my lessons and consequences of my inability to follow the Universal laws. I also understand and accept that the Universe wants me to realize all my talents and potentials, follow my life purpose and live to the fullest because through doing so I multiply the diversity, the goodness, the joy, and the love in this world. Remember, I had the purpose before anyone had an opinion about it.

These mantras should help you transcend your self-doubt and get you back to the inspired and excited state in a relatively short time span. Others will always try to shake your confidence because they themselves do not possess conviction in their abilities. Letting the opinion of people, who lack belief in their own values, make an impact on your psyche is not only foolish but could also lead you to trouble in the near future. Remember from our previous chapters- who is a fan and who is a player?

Focus On The Process, Not The Results

The second strategy involves taking a wider perspective of life and truly live in the flow. As Osho famously quoted in one of his speeches, *"Don't try to seek, search, knock, demand... instead, try to relax, relaxing will get you there, relaxing will help you achieve it, and most of all relaxing will help you vibrate with the Universal energies."* In both erotic and spiritual aspects of our lives, the key is to enjoy the moment. The second we start concentrating too heavily on the results, we find ourselves using the limbic part of our brain that is responsible for fight or flight responses, and start judging ourselves against the results (which will often make us feel like a failure).

Sex, in the modern world, has transgressed from a spiritual experience to a performance model or criterion, with an orgasm as its main prize. Many times, people suffer from sexual dysfunction only because they are not able to orgasm the *"right way"* or outperform their partner in a supposed sex-induced race.

But when we relax into the experience of intimacy, we can experience much more profound happiness. Orgasms in actuality transfer our physical bodies into a vessel of energy.

During orgasm, our body's cellular structure dissipates and our experiences try to connect us with the spiritual or source energy. Studies have proven that one of twenty individuals have experienced a transcendental orgasm characterized by shifts in space and time, timelessness and emptiness, a sensation of electrically illuminated bodies and transformation of the self, to name just a few. Those who are exposed to spiritual awakening through transcendent orgasm face a life-changing experiencing altogether. They no longer have the same views, and open their mind to new realities.

An orgasm is perhaps the most common and fruitful option when it comes to achieving spiritual bliss and numerous studies have supported its physical, mental and emotional benefits. Even the French term *"le petit mort"* accurately defines the spiritual implications of an orgasm as it translates to 'small death'. This small death highlights the process of eliminating our ego-driven self and connecting with each other and the divine more efficiently.

> *"The pleasure of living and the pleasure of the orgasm are identical, extreme orgasm anxiety forms the basis of the general fear of life."*
>
> **-Wilhelm Reich**

As soon as we find our spiritual purpose, your spiritual G-spot,- we transcend into an experience that shakes our core foundation as mortal entities. This resembles the same experience when we orgasm and cement our connection with the source energy. Time literally stops as we practice both these functions, and we become 100% authentic beings with no superficial features or actions attached to our existence.

Our body armor is shattered and it breaks away our ego, facades, society and cultural bonds; thereby becoming equal members of nature once again. There is no past or future when we feel these sensations; only the present moment exists. In these short blissful periods of silence, we arrive at a space or area that connects us to something greater than ourselves. We are able to connect with the divine flow of energy, our hearts and our very soul.

The more we dive into this sensation, the more experiences we have of creating, appearing, healing, regenerating, releasing, connecting, and understanding our very consciousness. In short, we are connected to an infinite number of possibilities. This ecstatic sensation allows us to enter planes that we are oblivious to, simply because our heart and soul are connected in perfect harmony. That is what the real G-spot of your soul feels like. I cannot wait for you to experience it.

****

s

It is 7 a.m., the alarm has gone off and I am stretching in my bed with a smile on my face. I don't have to get up as there is no job waiting for me in a stuffy office, no traffic jam is ready to steal my happiness and no cranky boss is about to destroy my self-esteem. I can stay in bed as long as I want to… But I cannot wait to get up and start my day… Creating, fulfilling, living, experiencing, enjoying, playing, living in the very G-spot of my soul- my life purpose. I wish all of you, my dear friends, to feel like this every morning… And I hope this book will help you on that incredible journey.

Bibliography

Burton, N. (2014). The Psychology of Masochism. *Psychology Today.* Retrieved from: https://www.psychologytoday.com/us/blog/ hide-and-seek/201408/the-psychology-sadomasochism

Dutton, D. G. & Aron, A. P. (1974). Some evidence for heightened sexual attraction under conditions of high anxiety.*Journal of Personality and Social Psychology.* 30 (4): 510–517

Karpman MD, Stephen (1968). Fairy tales and script drama analysis. *Transactional Analysis Bulletin.* 26 (7): 39–43.

Kashdan, T. & Biswas-Diener, R. (2015) The Upside of Your Dark Side.

Leknes, S & Tracey, I (2008). A common neurobiology for pain and pleasure. *Science & Society.* 9 p 314-320

Rozin, P. (1990). Getting to like the burn of chili pepper: Biological, psychological and cultural perspectives. In B. G. Green, J. R. Mason & M. R. Kare (Eds.), *Chemical senses,* Vol 2: Irritation. pp. 231–269. New York, NY: Marcel Dekker.

Rozin, P., et al. (2003) Glad to be sad. *Judgement and Decision Making.* Vol 8. No 4. pp. 439-447.

Schreiner, M (2018). Sadism. *Evolution Counseling.* Retrieved from: https://evolutioncounseling.com/sadism

Printed in the United States
By Bookmasters